Old Catholic

Old Catholic

✦

History, Ministry, Faith & Mission

Andre' Queen

iUniverse, Inc.
New York Lincoln Shanghai

Old Catholic
History, Ministry, Faith & Mission

iUniverse, Inc.

For information address:
iUniverse, Inc.
2021 Pine Lake Road, Suite 100
Lincoln, NE 68512
www.iuniverse.com

ISBN: 0-595-28407-8

Printed in the United States of America

The Old Catholic Church of the United States

Certain historical vignettes and historical information were provided, by permission, by The Archives of the American Congregation of St. Benedict through Bishop Donald Pierce Weeks, OSB, Abbot-Ordinary, and from the Old Catholic Church of America, through Archbishop-Metropolitan James Bostwick. Special thanks also goes to Archbishop Denis M. Garrison, for allowing the reproduction of his, Treatise on the Married Episcopate, An Argument From Tradition For Ordaining Married Priests To The Episcopate of the Orthodox Catholic Church.

To the Old Catholics of the continent of America in the Diaspora, laboring and praying daily in the service of Almighty God. This is dedicated to you for doing what others have said cannot be done. This is dedicated to the priest who, at this very moment is saying Mass on a makeshift altar, for the forgotten and rejected few. This is dedicated to the monks of the abbey taking in and caring for the "invisible minority" in anonymity and humility. This is dedicated to the bishops who have labored and cared for the people in their charge, who know every member of their church by name, and have felt the joys and the pains of shepherding them. This is dedicated to the laity, those to whom the clergy have pledged to serve in the name of God, those brave men and women who made the choice.

To my Archbishop, Robert M. Gubala, who puts up with my incessant chatter. To +Robert and +Anthony in the United Kingdom, and the entire English Catholic Church, who have been so greatly blessed.

To +Elijah, who reads my incessant email chatter, and held my hand through the development of this book. And to +Denis and Abbot Weeks, for allowing me to pick their brain. To many others (and you know who you are) who have been there for me along the way.

To the peacemakers and those working towards unity in the greater Old Catholic community, whose love and patience in this great work has borne fruit, and will bear even more.

To the fathers of the Old Catholic Church in the Americas, who sacrificed so much for the future of the Church. This is dedicated to their struggle and hardship, giving their entire adult lives to the church they loved so much. They faced ridicule, attack and viciousness for their choice, but chose to carry on, offering their suffering, many times at the hands of their episcopal peers of other denominations, up to God. They will never be forgotten.

To you, the reader for taking the first step.

And most of all to my family, who have been supportive and understanding throughout my ministry. My wife, Maria, qualifies for a special kind of clergy's wife sainthood, as she has endured much as a result of this ministry. To my children, Andre', Elizabeth and Matthew, the apple of their father's eye. To all of my family, I love you and you bring me great joy.

Contents

Foreword

The history of the Old Catholic Church's existence in the United States is one of the best kept secrets of our time. In all truth, the Old Catholic Church has enjoyed quite a rich history that is just being revealed to many.

Most of this history unfolds with the archeological skills, expertise and passion of the Most Reverend Andre' J.W. Queen, Old Catholic Bishop of Chicago and the author of this book. Many countless hours have been spent by Bishop Queen poring over historical documents and researching histories and biographies to make this factual publication a reality. This work is testament to Bishop Queen's love of his God and his Church.

The history of the Old Catholic Church in America is not without its critics, but like it or not the Church in its long history has made it's mark on Catholic Society over the last hundred plus years.

With Pioneers like Rene Vilatte and Arnold Harris Mathew, the foundation was laid for a Church that was not unlike the Roman Church in many of its theological views, but different in it discipline.

In this book you will learn of the History, Mission and the Theology, believed by Bishops Vilatte and Mathew, and countless others throughout the last century. These are the truths that these men struggled to present to the World of Catholics. Unlike many of their modern day successors these men tried to remain true to the meaning of being an "Old Catholic" and presented to the World a faith that we in the Old Catholic Church of the United States proclaim "Always, Everywhere and by All."

The Old Catholic Movement was borne out of a Papal decree in 1145 by Blessed Pope Eugene III, which gave the Cathedral Chapter of the See of Utrecht the right to elect its own successors when vacancies occured. This led to many problems with succeeding Pontiffs and their Curias. The rest of this story is historically narrated in the subsequent pages of this book.

I hope this book will be blessing upon your heart and that you will treasure it always. I know I will.

Peace and Blessings!

+Robert

Most Reverend
Robert Matthew Gubala, DD, Ph.D.
Archbishop-Metropolitan
Old Catholic Church of the US

Introduction

✦

"Who Do You Say I Am?"

Ten people will probably give you fifteen answers to this question if asked in regards to Old Catholics. Particularly in the Americas, where, as a denomination, it is not as well known as its European cousins in the Utrecht Union. But the theology of the American Old Catholic Churches is markedly different than that of the Utrecht Union Churches.

Throughout the decades, historians, theologians, and the curious all have written their own observations and opinions about what they felt Old Catholics were all about. Many of these literary works had a particular discriminatory flavor in favor of the writer's own religious affiliation, to the detriment of Old Catholics written about. Some of the books written were tools used to further discredit individuals within the Old Catholic movement, or to highlight their foibles in living color.

To be sure, the founders of Old Catholicism here were not perfect people; they made mistakes and at times suffered lapses in judgment. However, they strove to establish autocephalous Catholic parishes in the Americas against overwhelming odds, verbal and sometimes physical attack, and the monolithic wealth, influence and power of officials in the Roman Catholic Church, the Protestant Episcopal Church of the USA, and the Old Catholic Churches of the Utrecht Union, which eventually turned on their own.

Old Catholics in America today exist due to the efforts of these men, and those in the generations immediately afterwards, who continued the struggle. Splintered, and oftentimes isolated, Old Catholic parishes exist as an oasis to those who have been hurt and seek healing. Whereas it had been said that no one is born an Old Catholic, that is no longer true, and as the movement solidifies and parishes find one another, the Old Catholic movement in the Americas moves closer to realizing its full potential.

1

To understand what Old Catholics in the Americas *are*, it is important to understand what they are not. Old Catholics *are not* sedevacantists; they do not claim that the See of Peter is vacant. Old Catholics are *not* the product of rejection of Vatican II, nor are they a part of the "liberal reform" movement within the Roman Catholic Church. Likewise, Old Catholics are not gnostics or theosophists. Inversely, this means that individuals who are part of any of these groups, are *not* Old Catholic, regardless of superfluous claims. Old Catholics have a faith and identity all their own, that is based on Catholic theology, sans innovation, exclusion or outside influence.

1

What Is The Old Catholic Church?

The Old Catholics are a body of Christians committed to the Person of Jesus Christ and His teaching. We accept and believe the testimony of His Apostles, eyewitnesses of His Life, Death and Resurrection from among the dead. They passed on to succeeding generations their own testimony about Jesus Christ and His life. By the proclaiming of His Gospel, and the giving of their own testimony (called the Apostolic Tradition), the Church, which the Lord instituted, was built up. Old Catholics are a historic part of the One, Holy, Catholic and Apostolic Church and have their origins in the Ancient Catholic Church of the Netherlands. The Old Catholic Church in the Americas bears its Apostolic lineage from the Ancient Catholic Church of the Netherlands, the Syrian Orthodox (Oriental) Church of Antioch, and the Russian Orthodox Church. We will examine the traditions of the Western and Eastern lineage herein. The Old Catholic Church has its beginnings in the Roman Catholic Church, within the Kingdom of the Netherlands, about two hundred and seventy nine years ago.

The Ancient Catholic Church of the Netherlands

The area of Europe known as the Low Countries was missionized by St. Willibrord in the Seventh Century firmly establishing the Catholic Faith and Tradition in the Netherlands and other countries in that region. Early on, three principal dioceses were established in the cities of Utrecht, Deventer and Haarlem to administer the affairs of the Church in the territory. Utrecht eventually became the archiepiscopal see with supervision over Deventer and Haarlem. Assenting to a petition made by the Holy Roman Emperor Conrad III and Bishop Heribert of Utrecht, Blessed Pope Eugene III, in 1145 A.D. granted the Cathedral Chapter of Utrecht the right to elect successors to the See in times of vacancy. This right was later extended to include three additional collegial

3

churches.[1] This privilege was confirmed by the fourth Council of the Lateran in 1215.

The autonomous character of the Ancient Catholic Church in the Netherlands was further demonstrated when a second grant by Pope Leo X, Debitum Pastoralis, conceded to Philip of Burgundy, 57th Bishop of Utrecht, that neither he nor his successors, nor any of their clergy or laity, should ever, in the first instance, have his cause evoked to any external tribunal, not even under pretense of any apostolic letters whatever; and that all such proceedings should be, ipso facto, null and void. This papal concession, in 1520, was of the greatest importance in defense of the rights of the Church.

The Church in the Netherlands and the Reformation

Armed with the protection of the papal concessions, the Church in the Netherlands continued to minister even through the Reformation. During this period of strife, the Church in the Netherlands, as in many other countries, was forced to "go underground" in order to survive. But survive and remain extant, it did. Eventually, the Archbishop of Utrecht and other Church leaders reached an informal agreement with the civil government, whereby it could again function openly without interference from the Reformers.

The Archbishop of Utrecht and the Dutch Catholic Church, being used to a more austere form of worship and being Catholics at peril, sympathized with members of the European Jansenist Catholic movement, and incurred the wrath of the Jesuits as a result. "Jansenism" was a movement within the Roman Catholic Church that preferred a rigorous piety on Catholic expression, acceptance of predestination, and an emphasis on the sinfulness of man. The underlying theology that Jansenism was based upon, was the work *Augustinus*, written by Bishop of Ypres, Cornelius Jansen.

Jansen wrote his work based upon an intense study of the theology of St. Augustine of Hippo and entrusted his writings to trusted friends to be published after his death. The extreme expression of his work was termed "Jansenism". Five theological propositons, said to have been those of Jansen, were condemned as heresy in the Papal Bull, "*Cum occasione*" on June 8, 1653. [2]

Members of the Church were then required to sign an affirmation of a formulary condemning the five propositions, claiming that they had all been part of Cornelius Jansen's work *Augustinus*, but in fact were not. This caused a rejection of the formulary by both Jansenists and non-Jansenists alike within the Church, based upon the inconsistency of the facts. All five of these propositions were not found within Jansen's work *Augustinus*. The formulary was also rejected by others who had not read the work in question, but were, nonetheless, prevailed upon to sign the formulary condemning it. Signing the formulary would be asserting that the Five Propositions were found within Augustinus, failure to sign it would bring excommunication, treating the entire issue as a matter of faith. This was considered to be a situation in which the Pope was imposing a new dogma on the faithful, without the consent of a general Church Council. This caused rejection from nationalists, holders of Gallican Principals, and Jansenists due to the doctrinal concerns. [3]

On September 8th 1713, Pope Clement XI issued the bull "Unigenitus", condemning 101 propositions in a treatise by French Jansenist, Pasquier Quesnel (1634-1719) entitled *Moral Reflexions on the New Testatment*.

When the Jesuit Order first entered the Netherlands in 1592, the differences in policy were immediately apparent, between them and the historic Church of the Netherlands, in that the Jesuit Order sought to consolidate all canonical authority in the office of the Pope, and the local Church which had the ancient rights, canonically possessed, to elect its own successors to the local bishoprics. The local people found themselves in a power struggle between the Jesuits consolidating authority for the Pope, who demanded unswerving loyalty, and the King of Spain, who likewise demanded unswerving loyalty.

The Archdiocese of Utrecht, along with Haarlem and Deventer, were under siege by the Jesuit Order, for refusing to give up the right to freely elect Episcopal successors. This condition resulted in numerous problems, which, at times, required Congregations of the Church to decide. The Chapter of Utrecht understood the Church to be a confederacy, on which local segments of the Church had certain rights and privileges which were irrevocable (Gallicanism). The Jesuits understood the Church to be a hierarchical monarchy, with the Pope as its absolute head.

With respect to the intrigue of Jansenism, many within the local Church would not sign a formulary which was inaccurate, and regarding a written work that many had not read. In addition, most of the local Church clergy had been trained at Louvain, and had been in contact with members of the Jansenist Party, whose leaders took refuge and sought protection in Holland. [4] In addition, differences in piety, between the Dutch Church and the Jesuits only served to emphasize their underlying differences. The Dutch Church was of a more austere piety, and the Dutch Calvinist Government preferred a local Dutch Episcopacy, rather than a foreign bishop appointed by Rome. Attempts at reconciliation failed, as Rome was adamant that the local Church give up its ancient rights and privileges, deny the existence of the Chapters, sign the Formulary and accept centralized leadership from the vicar-apostolic. In addition, the chapter was without a bishop to ordain priests, as none of the bishops outside of the Netherlands wished to incur the punishment of Rome for supporting the local Dutch Church.

And so, the Dutch Church was forced, by necessity, to function as a separate Catholic communion. Dominique Marie Varlet, Bishop of Babylon, while traveling incognito under orders from Rome to his new See, consented to confirm children for the Dutch Church, and continued his journey to Persia. He was later formally suspended from his office by the *Congregation for the Propagation of the Faith* for failing to adhere to the Bull "Ungenitus" and for not obtaining permission to perform episcopal functions in the Netherlands (which he could not have obtained traveling, under orders from Rome, incognito). The Bishop traveled back to Europe, stopping in Amsterdam to prepare his defense, and continuing to France. Due to his unwillingness to accept "Ungenitus" or apologize for having confirmed the children, he was informed that his defense would fail. He then returned to Holland, to prepare a more comprehensive defense of his actions. While there, he was prevailed upon by the Chapters to, under their lawful right of election, to consecrate bishops for them without papal consent, which he did.

On October 15, 1724, Cornelius van Steenoven was consecrated the seventh Archbishop of Utrecht by Dominique Marie Varlet, Bishop of Babylon, without the authority or Apostolic Mandate of the Pope, marking the beginning of an independent Old Roman Catholic Church of Holland.

The Move from Isolation

Following the First Vatican Council in 1870 (at which the hierarchy of the Church of Holland were refused admittance), a considerable dissent among Catholics, especially in Germany, Austria and Switzerland, arose over the dogma of papal infallibility. The dissenters, while holding the Church in General Council to be infallible, could not accept the proposition that the Pope, acting alone, in matters of faith and morals is infallible. Many formed independent communities that came to be known as "Old Catholic". They are called "Old Catholics" because they sought to adhere to the beliefs and practices of the Catholic Church of the post-Apostolic era and the theology of the Church prior to the Vatican Council. The Old Catholic communities appealed to the Archbishop of Utrecht who consecrated the first bishops for these communities. Eventually, under the leadership of the Church of Holland, these Old Catholic communities joined together to form the Utrecht Union of Churches. The Utrecht Union of Churches approbated, in 1908, the establishment of a mission in Great Britain. Archbishop Gerardus Gul of Utrecht consecrated Father Arnold Harris Mathew, a resigned Roman Catholic priest, Regionary Bishop for England. It was Bishop Mathew's charge to minister among Anglo-Catholics and Roman Catholics impeded from full participation in the life and sacraments of the Church. Toward this end, Bishop Mathew consecrated Austrian nobleman, Prince Rudolph Edward de Landes Berghes, in 1913 for work in Scotland. Prince Rudolph (1873-1920) left England for the United States at the onset of World War I.

Bishop Mathew, seeing the changes within the Utrecht Union of Old Catholic Churches, and a leaning towards greater communion with the Anglican Communion, which encouraged a steady rejection of uniquely "Catholic" expressions of faith, theology and worship not found within Anglican theology, withdrew from the Utrecht Union.

The Most Reverend Arnold Harris Mathew
The Declaration of Autonomy[5]

We the undersigned Bishop, on behalf of our clergy and laity of the Catholic Church of England, hereby proclaim and declare the autonomy and independence of our portion of the One, Holy, Catholic and Apostolic Church. We are in no way whatever subject to or dependent upon any foreign See, nor do we recognize the right of any members of the religious bodies known as 'Old Catholics' on the Continent, to require submission from us to their authority or jurisdiction, or the decrees, decisions, rules or assemblies, in which we have neither taken part nor expressed agreement.

We had supposed and believed that the Faith, once delivered to the Saints, and set forth in the decrees of the Councils accepted as Ecumenical no less in the West than in the East, would have continued unimpaired, whether by augmentation or by diminution, in the venerable Church of the Dutch Nation.

We anticipated that the admirable fidelity with which the Bishops and Clergy of that Church had adhered to the Faith and handed it down, untarnished by heresy, notwithstanding grievous persecution during so many centuries, would never have wavered.

Unfortunately, however, we discover with dismay, pain, and regret that the standards of orthodoxy, laid down of old by the Fathers and Councils of the East and West alike, having been departed from in various particulars by certain sections of Old Catholicism, these departures, instead of being checked and repressed, are, at least tacitly, tolerated and acquiesced in without protest, by the Hierarchy of the Church of the Netherlands.

In order to avoid misapprehension, we here specify nine of the points of difference between Continental Old Catholics and ourselves:

(1) Although the Synod of Jerusalem, held under Dositheus in 1672, was not an Ecumenical Council, its decrees are accepted by the Holy Orthodox Church of the Orient as accurately expressing its belief, and are in harmony with the decrees of the Council of Trent on the dogmas of which they treat. We are in agreement with the Holy Orthodox Church, regarding this Synod, Hence, we hold and declare that there are Seven Holy Mysteries or Sacraments instituted by Our Divine Lord and Saviour Jesus Christ, therefore all of them necessary for the sal-

vation of mankind, though all are not necessarily to be received by every individual, e.g. Holy Orders and Matrimony. Certain sections, if not all, of the Old Catholic bodies, reject this belief and refuse to assent to the decrees of the Holy Synod of Jerusalem.

(2) Moreover, some of them have abolished the Sacrament of Penance by condemning and doing away with auricular confession; others actively discourage this salutary practice; others, again, whilst tolerating its use, declare the Sacrament of Penance to be merely optional, therefore unnecessary, and of no obligation, even for those who have fallen into mortal sin after Baptism.

(3) In accordance with the belief and practice of the Universal Church, we adhere to the doctrine of the Communion of Saints by invoking and venerating the Blessed Virgin Mary, and those who have received the crown of glory in heaven, as well as the Holy Angels of God. The Old Catholics in the Netherlands have not yet altogether abandoned this pious and helpful custom, but, in some other countries, invocation of the Saints has been totally abolished by the Old Catholics.

(4) Although it may be permissible and, indeed, very desirable, in some countries, and' under certain circumstances, to render the Liturgy into the vernacular languages, we consider it to be neither expedient nor tolerable that individuals should compose new liturgies, according to their own particular views, or make alterations, omissions and changes in venerable rites to suit their peculiar fancies, prejudices or idiosyncrasies. We lament the mutilations of this kind which have occurred among the Old Catholics in several countries and regret that no two of the new liturgies composed and published by them are alike, either in form or in ceremony. In all of them the ancient rubrics have been set aside, and the ceremonies and symbolism with which the Sacred Mysteries of the Altar have been reverently environed for many centuries, have, either wholly or in part, been ruthlessly swept away. The Rite of Benediction of the Blessed Sacrament has also been almost universally abolished among the Old Catholics.

(5) In accordance with the primitive teaching of the Church of the Netherlands, which prevailed until a very recent date, we consider it a duty on the part of Western Christians to remember His Holiness the Pope as their Patriarch in their prayers and sacrifices. The name of His Holiness should, therefore, retain its position in the Canon of the Mass, where, as we observed at our consecration in Utrecht, it was customary, and remained so until a recent date in the present year

(1910), for the celebrant to recite the name of our Patriarch in the usual manner in the Mass and in the Litany of the Saints. The publication of a new vernacular Dutch Liturgy in the present year causes us to regret that the clergy of Holland are now required to omit the name of His Holiness in the Canon of the Mass. Happily, only a small number of other alterations in the text of the Canon have, so far, been introduced. These include the omission of the title, 'ever Virgin' whenever it occurs in the Latin Missal. Such alterations pave the way for others of an even more serious nature, which may be made in the future, and, as we think, are to be deplored.

(6) Following the example of our Catholic forefathers, we venerate the adorable Sacrifice of the Mass as the supreme act of Christian worship instituted by Christ Himself. We grieve that the Old Catholic clergy, in most countries, have abandoned the daily celebration Of Mass, and now limit the offering the Christian Sacrifice to Sundays and a few of the greater Feasts. The corresponding neglect of the Blessed Sacrament, and infrequency of Holy Communion, on the part of the laity, are marked.

(7) In accordance with Catholic custom and with the decrees of the Ecumenical Councils, we hold that the honor and glory of God are promoted and increased by the devout and religious use of holy pictures, statues, symbols, relics, and the like, as aids to devotion, and that, in relations to those they represent, they are to be held in veneration. The Old Catholics have, generally speaking, preferred to dispense with such helps to piety.

(8) We consider that the Holy Sacraments should be administered only to those who are members of the Holy Catholic Church, not only by Baptism, but by the profession of the Catholic Faith in its integrity. Unhappily, we find persons who are not Catholics are now admitted to receive Holy Communion in all Old Catholic places of worship on the Continent.

(9) The Old Catholics have ceased to observe the prescribed days of fasting and abstinence, and no longer observe the custom of receiving Holy Communion fasting.

For these and other reasons, which it is unnecessary to detail, we, the undersigned Bishop, desire, by these presents, to declare our autonomy and our independence of all foreign interference in our doctrine, discipline and policy. *In necessaries unites, in dubiis libertes, in omnibus caritas.*

+Arnold Harris Mathew

December 29, 1910

The Feast of St. Thomas of Canterbury

In the United States

Bishop de Landes Berghes, in spite of great difficulty and isolation from the Utrecht Union of Churches, due to Bishop Mathew withdrawing from the Union, was able to plant the roots of an independent expression of Catholicism in America. He elevated to the episcopacy two priests, Carmel Henry Carfora and William Francis Brothers. Each of these bishops, in his own manner, continued the mission begun by Bishop de Landes Berghes. With the passing of these original organizers from the ecclesiastical scene, the Old Catholic Church in the United States has evolved from a fairly centralized administration with structured oversight of ministry to a local and regional model of administration with self-governing dioceses and provinces more closely following St. Ignatius of Antioch's concepts of the Church as a communion of communities each laboring together to proclaim the message of the Gospel.

Another Old Catholic priest, Fr. Joseph Renee Vilatte, began his ministry in Wisconsin, which led to the establishment of Old Catholic familial lines making us brothers and sisters to the Oriental Orthodox Churches in Middle East.

Fr. Vilatte was ordained an Old Catholic deacon and priest in Berne, Switzerland by Old Catholic Bishop Edward Herzog in 1885, for Old Catholic parishes in Wisconsin. He enjoyed the support of the Episcopal Bishop John Brown of Fond Du Lac, Wisconsin. [6] Churches were built for the French immigrants he served in several parishes that grew and thrived.

Upon the death of his benefactor, Bishop Brown, a successor, Bishop Charles Grafton, was appointed. Bishop Grafton was opposed to the autocephalous nature of the Old Catholic parishes and sought to bring them under his authority. The parishes assembled in synod and elected Fr. Vilatte to be consecrated as bishop for their Old Catholic parishes, placing themselves at odds with Bishop Grafton. This increased the animus between Bishop Grafton and the Old Catholic parishes of Duval, Gardner and Menominee, in the person of their new bishop-elect, Fr. Vilatte.

The conflict set into motion caused Bishop Grafton to state his case to the Old Catholic Bishops of Europe who initially had thought to consider the consecration of Fr. Vilatte at their next Congress, but upon the report of Bishop Grafton, decided not to. They did instruct Fr. Vilatte to separate his parishes from interaction with the Episcopal Diocese, which left the small body vulnerable to the ecclesiastical powers that existed, and further exacerbated Bishop Grafton. Fr. Vilatte placed the parishes under the protection of the Russian Orthodox bishop Vladimir (Sokolovsky), of the Diocese of Alaska, who received them warmly. The church trustees became aware of an autocephalous Church of India, and requested its assistance in consecrating their bishop-elect. [7]

Fr. Vilatte ultimately became Bishop Vilatte, consecrated bishop under the authority of Mar Ignatius Peter III, Patriarch of Antioch, of the Syrian Orthodox Church. He was consecrated a bishop by Mar Julius, Metropolitan of the Independent Catholic Church of Ceylon, Goa and India, (venerated as a saint by the Malankaran Orthodox Syrian Church of India after his passing) who was assisted by Mar Paul Athanasius, Bishop of Kottayam and Mar Gregorius Geevargheese, Bishop of Niranam (who was later canonized a Saint by the Malankaran Orthodox Syrian Church of India) on May 29, 1892 according to the Roman Pontifical. He then returned to the United States, where his Episcopal lines would stand alongside those of Bishop Mathew, in securing valid lines of Apostolic Succession, both of which the Old Catholic Church in the Americas posses.

Old Catholicism in the Americas

"Old Catholic" and "Old Roman Catholic" are terms used to identify Old Catholic churches and parishes in the United States who are not necessarily affiliated with ethnic Old Catholic communities such as the Polish National Catholic Church. The original diocese established by the late Archbishop Carfora in the 1920's in Chicago was called the Old Roman Catholic Diocese in the United States. Old Catholic Theology and Holy Orders in the United States and Canada flow primarily from the work and influence of Archbishops Arnold Mathew and Joseph Renee Vilatte. Because of this, nearly all of our Catholic communities are called "Old Catholic" or "Old Roman Catholic". The theology of Old Catholics in the United States differs from that of the European Old Catholic Churches of the Utrecht Union, as most of the Old Catholic Churches of the Utrecht Union were formed as a reaction against Vatican I. Old Catholic Churches of the United States tend to be traditionally more Roman in expressions of faith and worship than our European cousins, and hold fast to theological expressions of faith that the European Churches reject or minimize. In addition, the American Church has accepted an infusion of Eastern Orthodox and Oriental theology and apostolic lineage.

What Old Catholics Believe

The faith of Old Catholics is simply that of the Catholic Church as taught by the Church from apostolic times to the present day. The Oecumenical Councils clearly express what Old Catholics believe without the need for apology or excuse. In 1823, Archbishop Willibrord van Os of Utrecht reiterated adherence to the unchanging doctrine of Catholicism in the following words: "We accept without any exception whatever, all the Articles of the Holy Catholic Faith. We will never hold nor teach, now or afterwards, any other opinions than those that have been decreed, determined and published by our Mother, Holy Church…" Thus, Old Catholics, tracing their Apostolic Succession through the Roman Catholic Church to the Apostles, participated in the full sacramental ministry of the Church. The Rule of Faith of Old Catholics is faithful adherence to Sacred Scripture and the Apostolic Tradition. The crystallized expression of faith of the Old Catholic Churches of the Utrecht Union was formed in the "Declaration of Utrecht".

The Declaration of Utrecht, 1889[8]
of the Old Catholic Bishops of the Netherlands, Germany and Switzerland

1. We adhere faithfully to the Rule of Faith laid down by St. Vincent of Lerins in these terms: "Id teneamus, quod ubique, quod semper, quod ab omnibus creditum est; hoc est etenim vere proprieque catholicum." For this reason we preserve in professing the faith of the primitive Church, as formulated in the oecumenical symbols and specified precisely by the unanimously accepted decisions of the Oecumenical Councils held in the undivided Church of the first thousand years.

2. We therefore reject the decrees of the so-called Council of the Vatican, which were promulgated July 18th, 1870, concerning the infallibility and the universal Episcopate of the Bishop of Rome, decrees which are in contradiction with the faith of the ancient Church, and which destroy its ancient canonical constitution by attributing to the Pope the plentitude of ecclesiastical powers over all Dioceses and over all the faithful. By denial of this primatial jurisdiction we do not wish to deny the historical primacy which several Oecumenical Councils and Fathers of the ancient Church have attributed to the Bishop of Rome by recognizing him as the Primus inter pares.

3. We also reject the dogma of the Immaculate Conception promulgated by Pius IX in 1854 in defiance of the Holy Scriptures and in contradiction to the tradition of the centuries.

4. As for other Encyclicals published by the Bishops of Rome in recent times for example, the Bulls Unigenitus and Auctorem fidei, and the Syllabus of 1864, we reject them on all such points as are in contradiction with the doctrine of the primitive Church, and we do not recognize them as binding on the consciences of the faithful. We also renew the ancient protests of the Catholic Church of Holland against the errors of the Roman Curia, and against its attacks upon the rights of national Churches.

5. We refuse to accept the decrees of the Council of Trent in matters of discipline, and as for the dogmatic decisions of that Council we accept them only so far as they are in harmony with the teaching of the primitive Church.

6. Considering that the Holy Eucharist has always been the true central point of Catholic worship, we consider it our right to declare that we maintain with per-

fect fidelity the ancient Catholic doctrine concerning the Sacrament of the Altar, by believing that we receive the Body and Blood of our Saviour Jesus Christ under the species of bread and wine. The Eucharistic celebration in the Church is neither a continual repetition nor a renewal of the expiatory sacrifice which Jesus offered once for all upon the Cross: but it is a sacrifice because it is the perpetual commemoration of the sacrifice offered upon the Cross, and it is the act by which we represent upon earth and appropriate to ourselves the one offering which Jesus Christ makes in Heaven, according to the Epistle to the Hebrews 9:11-12, for the salvation of redeemed humanity, by appearing for us in the presence of God (Heb. 9:24). The character of the Holy Eucharist being thus understood, it is, at the same time, a sacrificial feast, by means of which the faithful in receiving the Body and Blood of our Saviour, enter into communion with one another (I Cor. 10:17).

7. We hope that Catholic theologians, in maintaining the faith of the undivided Church, will succeed in establishing an agreement upon questions which have been controverted ever since the divisions which arose between the Churches. We exhort the priests under our jurisdiction to teach, both by preaching and by the instruction of the young, especially the essential Christian truths professed by all the Christian confessions, to avoid, in discussing controverted doctrines, any violation of truth or charity, and in word and deed to set an example to the members.

8. By maintaining and professing faithfully the doctrine of Jesus Christ, by refusing to admit those errors which by the fault of men have crept into the Catholic Church, by laying aside the abuses in ecclesiastical matters, together with the worldly tendencies of the hierarchy, we believe that we shall be able to combat efficaciously the great evils of our day, which are unbelief and indifference in matters of religion.

Utrecht, 24th September 1889

+Heykamp
+Rinkel
+Diependaal
+Reinkens
+Herzog

How Do We Differ From The Roman Catholic Church?

In matters of discipline, administration and procedure, Old Catholics differ from the Roman Catholic Church. For example, clerical celibacy (which is a matter of discipline) is optional among Old Catholics. Married men may be ordained into the Holy Priesthood. Liturgical expression is also a matter of discipline determined by the local bishop. Consequently, many Old Catholic communities use the current Roman Rite, others utilize the Old Catholic Missal and Ritual of 1909 by Archbishops Arnold Mathew and Gerardus Gul, while others maintain Tridentine liturgy, in Latin or direct translation into classical or modern English, in those parishes that desire it. Eastern Rite Old Catholic parishes exist as well, which follow the ancient liturgies of that rich tradition, including the Divine Liturgies of St. John Chrystosom, St. Basil and St. James. Because Old Catholic communities are small, they are able to successfully implement the Ignatian model of the Church referred to earlier. This concept views the faithful with their clergy and bishop as a community or family in loving concern for each other and each working together to live the Scriptural commands in their daily lives as Christians bringing the love of Christ to others. Old Catholic communities utilize their size and lack of highly detailed structure to the very best advantage organizationally by their ability to expedite decisions affecting the sacramental and community life of the faithful, within the revelation and authority of Holy Scripture and Apostolic Tradition. Old Catholic clergy generally remain at their initial parish of ordination for the duration of their sacramental ministry.

Other Distinctions

There are other differences by which Old Catholic communities are differentiated from Roman Catholic parishes. The matter of papal infallibility defined by Vatican Council I is a non-issue for Old Catholics, since they are not under papal jurisdiction. All Old Catholic communities accord the Holy Father that respect due him as Successor of St. Peter, Prince of the Apostles and Patriarch of the West. Old Catholics adhere to the teaching from apostolic times that the Church in General Council is infallible. Another difference is that divorced people who remarry are treated in a pastoral manner and not excluded from the sacramental life of the Church. Further, the matter of contraception is treated as a matter of personal conscience between husband and wife (abortion is expressly prohibited). Old Catholic theology recognizes that the Church's teaching magisterium has no less than two objects: the formation of conscience, in which case authority has an instructive quality; and the nurturing of a formed conscience to full maturity, in which case authority is guiding but not directive.

Old Catholic Communities in the Americas are different in theology from their European cousins, not having been formed in the heat of the Reformation and reaction to Vatican I. American Old Catholics tend to maintain particularly historical Catholic liturgies, with little or no change. Many use the Tridentine vestments and liturgical expressions, and the parishes have a "catholicity" that is markedly "older" than that found in many Roman Catholic Churches today. This tends to be a common theme among American Old Catholics.

ENDNOTES FOR CHAPTER ONE

[1.] J. M. Neale, *A History of the So-called Jansenist Church of Holland*, (Oxford, London, 1857) p. 64.

[2.] Claude B. Moss, *The Old Catholic Movement*, (SPCK, London, 1964), p. 45.

[3.] Ibid, p.134-135.

[4.] Ibid, p.114.

[5.] Arnold Harris Mathew, "Declaration of Autonomy and Independence" *An Episcopal Odyssey*, November 1, 1915.

[6.] The Archives of the American Congregation of St. Benedict, Bishop Donald Pierce Weeks, OSB, Abbot-Ordinary. Used by permission, 2003.

[7.] Ibid.

[8.] The Old Catholic Bishops of the Netherlands, Germany and Switzerland, *The Declaration of Utrecht*, (1889)

2

The Old Catholic Churches in the Americas

By developing new methods and ideas with an emphasis on community, and Catholicism, which expresses a warmth and interest in the total person, Old Catholic communities are able to address the needs of today's society in the beginning years of the Twenty-First Century. American Old Catholicism is an understanding of the Western and Eastern traditions in one complete tradition. For the contemporary Catholic searching to maintain Traditional Faith but desiring to do so without excessive institutionalism that often loses contact with the individual; for those with a Catholic background who feel impeded from full participation in the life and Sacraments of the Church; for the many unchurched who desire the joy and peace of Our Lord's Word and His Holy Sacraments, Old Catholic communities provide a viable alternative and allow a person to be a part of Christ's Church, and be at peace with his/her conscience. Old Catholic communities, because of their size, can give individual attention to the individual spiritual needs of the faithful and, where necessary, develop unique ministries to meet those needs.

American Old Catholicism And What It Is Not

While it is true that the Old Catholics Church is independent of the Roman Catholic Communion, it is not independent of fundamental Catholic theology. It is not possible to actually be Old Catholic, and at the same time reject the foundational theology of Old Catholicism. When Archbishop Mathew withdrew from the Utrecht Union, he was withdrawing and separating himself from a Union, which had rejected the earlier positions of the Church at Utrecht, Holland, in favor of more Protestant theology. He was adhering to the Dutch Church's initial expression of faith as an autocephalous Catholic Church expressed at its inception as such in 1724, and rejecting the reactionary position

20

espoused by the newer Old Catholic Churches of Germany, Austria and Switzerland established in 1870 in response to Vatican I.[1]

Ultimately, the Dutch Church reversed its support of theological expressions found in the documents of the Council of Trent, joined the newer Old Catholic Churches of Europe in backing away from Transubstantiation, auricular confession, veneration of the saints, and other Catholic expressions of faith.[2] Archbishop Mathew found himself torn between staying in the Union which was steadily dismantling parts of its Catholic identity, and leaving it and stepping out into ecclesiastical oblivion in order to cling to the truth of the universal faith. He chose truth over comfort, and so must we.

It is not enough to claim to be Old Catholic, <u>one must live out the tenets of the faith in their life</u>, and cling tenaciously to it, rejecting the "Spirit of the Age", which seeks to minimalize, trivialize or destroy the faith. Holy Scripture instructs us in the Faith in a way we can see, Sacred Tradition instructs us in the way in which the Church lives out the teachings of Christ, as we have been taught by the Fathers, Teachers and Martyrs of the Church, as they have tried to imitate Christ in their lives. If we do not find a teaching within this Deposit of Faith, as expressed by the Magisterium of the Church, then it is not part of the Faith. Attempts to marry social and political concerns with the Church's expression of Faith and change the Deposit of Faith to "make it fit" current sociopolitical concepts is blasphemous and utterly sinful. Twenty-first century attempts to explain that "Jesus could not have done such-and-such, due to the social and political situation of the times..." is blasphemous and seeks to marginalize and minimalize Christ Jesus, who, as God, is all powerful, establishing His Church with such spiritual authority that the "gates of Hell shall not prevail against it". Attempts to remake God in our image belie rebellion in the heart of the individual, and a refusal to submit to God's authority.

The Establishment Of The Early Church

Throughout the Episcopal ministries of Archbishops Mathew, Vilatte and Rudolph Edward de Landes Berghes, many individuals from many different theological camps sought to discredit and ruin these men and the church they sought to establish. It is absolutely true that they did not, in all things and in all ways, make the best choices—however no one does. But, as their young parishes began to take root and grow, they oftentimes found themselves in the middle of a three-way ecclesiastical tug-of-war, with the Roman Catholic Church, the Protestant Episcopal Church and the Old Catholic Union of Utrecht Churches.

Joseph Renee Vilatte

Archbishop Vilatte, having raised funds and established parishes with the kindly assistance of the Episcopal Bishop of Fond Du Lac, Wisconsin, Bishop Brown, conversely was countered at every step by the bishop's successor, Bishop Grafton. Upon learning that the Old Catholic Bishops of Europe instructed Fr. Vilatte to separate himself and his parishes from the PECUSA, Bishop Grafton, seeing this as a challenged to what he thought was his right as bishop to govern and control, began a campaign to discredit Vilatte, so that not even the Old Catholic Bishops would want to eventually consecrate him a bishop, a necessity to ensure the autonomy of the Old Catholic Mission Parishes under the then Fr. Vilatte. This course of action being successful, the parish chapter prevailed upon the Independent (Jacobite Orthodox) Catholic Church of Ceylon, India to consecrate Fr. Vilatte. This too, Bishop Grafton attempted to sidetrack with a telegraph to Mar Julius. Fr. Vilatte, upon arrival in India, waited and underwent examination in excess of eight months. After due consultation with the Syrian Patriarch, the approval was given. Mar Julius, with the assistance of two bishops, did consecrate Joseph Renee Vilatte Archbishop of the Old Catholic Church of the Americas.[3]

This having been done, Bishop Grafton sought to claim that the orders were invalid, illicit and irregular, to which Mar Julius I and many others refuted. Over time, however, as Archbishop Vilatte traveled across the U.S, Canada and France, Bishop Grafton took possession of the parishes, churches and rectories in Wisconsin. Had the Archbishop the monetary funds to go to court, he would have been able to recoup much of the property, having been deeded specifically to his work there. Other parish property was lost forever to him, having been previously convinced to sign ownership over to the Bishop, before understanding the gravity of his error.

Archbishop Vilatte enabled, organized and ordained and consecrated clergy for the autocephalous Polish Catholic movement in the U.S. Churches were built, foundations laid and clergy ordained in Chicago, IL., Buffalo, NY and elsewhere in the U.S. The progress of the Polish Catholic Church was solidly moving forward, when the Old Catholic Bishops of the Utrecht Union consecrated a Bishop for a rival Polish Church in the United States (an individual rejected by Vilatte for the Episcopate), which decimated the Polish Catholic Church under Vilatte and became the precursor of the Polish National Catholic Church, the only U.S. member of the Utrecht Union.[4]

*[Decades later, the Polish National Catholic Church severed communion with the rest of the Utrecht Union Church, due to the European Old Catholics engaged in the attempted ordination of women to the priesthood.]

Arnold Matthew

Likewise, Archbishop Mathew found himself between the Churches of the Utrecht Union, the Roman Catholic Church and the Church of England, all seeking to discredit him and his work. Unwittingly giving fuel to the fire, he ordained an individual who appeared by his deportment to be an excellent candidate and later priest. Upon consecration to the episcopate, it was later found that he was a supporter of Theosophy. Although Archbishop Mathew attempted to excise this cancer from the Church in the UK, it was too late, and the ejection of this individual and his followers damaged the movement severely in the UK.

Rudolph Edward de Landes Berghes

Archbishop Rudolph Edward de Landes Berghes, likewise found opposition in the U.S., and owing to the war and cultural differences, Vilatte and De Landes Berghes were not able to unify their ministries into a single effort.

"Born of an aristocratic family in Naples, Italy (not far from the homes of Carmel H. Carfora and Al Capone) on November 1, 1873, he received his education at the best schools: Eaton, The University of Cambridge, Paris, Brussels, completing courses in law, Theology, Military Tactics, earning an LLB and Ph.D. He served as Captain in the Sudan on Lord Kitchner's staff and retired from the military with the rank of Lieutenant Colonel. Three years later, in the early part of 1912, through the agencies of two staunch supporters of Archbishop Mathews, deLandas Berghes met Mathew and the two formed a warm and lasting friendship." [5]

"The Austrian Nobleman, who was raised to the Episcopate by Bishop Arnold Harris Mathew on June 29, 1913 was known to the world as Rudolph Francis Edward St. Patrick Alphonsus Ghislain de Gramont Hamilton de Lorraine-Brabant, Prince de Landas Berghes et de Rache, Duc de St. Winock. The British Foreign Office arranged for his departure from England in September of 1914 to prevent his being interned during the war as an "enemy alien." Such an act would have been highly embarrassing since the Prince was related to nearly every royal house in Europe.

He came to America and, as was common in those days for many Old Catholic clergymen in America, was licensed to function in the Episcopal Church. He assisted in the consecration of Hiram Richard Hulse as the Protestant Episcopal Bishop of Cuba on January 12, 1915 as is record in the Episcopal Church Annual (c.f. 1953 Annual.)

Bishop Rudolph de Landas Berghes took up residence at St. Dunstan's Abbey, Waukegan, Illinois and raised Abbot William H. F. Brothers to the episcopacy on October 3, 1916. The following day he consecrated Carmel Henry Carfora as a bishop of the Old Roman Catholic Church of America. He, along with Bishop Carfora, consecrated Stanislaus Mickiewicz, a former Polish National Catholic priest, in 1917.

Two years later Bishop de Landas Berghes resigned and retired to an Augustinian monastery in Villanova, Pennsylvania where he was reconciled to the Holy See and where he died on November 17, 1920." [6]

Paul Francis Cope

Bishop Cope was consecrated by Archbishop James Bartholomew Ranks of London. He journeyed to America specifically for the purpose of establishing an Old Catholic Church here. The Old Catholic Church of America was officially launched in May 1925. [7]

Aftimos Ofiesh

The Russian Orthodox Church established missions in Alaska and Northern America. Bishop Aftimos Ofiesh was sent to America to establish the Orthodox faith there. He established what was to become the American Orthodox Church. Father Aftimios (Ofiesh) was consecrated by Abp. Evdokim in early months of 1917. Aftimios was elevated to archbishop by Metropolitan Platon in 1923.

On February 2, 1927, a solemn act was signed by Russian Orthodox Church officials, charging Abp. Aftimios *"with the full responsibility and duty of caring and providing for American Orthodoxy in the special sense of Orthodox Catholic People born in America and primarily of whatever nationality or linguistic character or derivation not satisfactorily provided with proper canonical Orthodox Catholic care..., or who may wish to attach themselves by the properly and legally provided means to an autonomous, independent, American Orthodox Catholic Church."*

This first attempt at an American Orthodox Church met with opposition from the various autocephalous Orthodox Churches and with little to no support from other ethnic churches in America. Abp. Aftimios married in 1933. He lived out the remainder of his life in virtual isolation. During his tenure, Abp. Aftimios consecrated at least two men to continue the work of the American Church. Emmanuel Abo Hatab was consecrated in 1927 for the See of Montreal, and Sophronius Bashira was consecrated in 1928 for the See of Los Angeles.

Theophan (Fan S. Noli)

Metropolitan Theophan (Fan S. Noli) of the Albanian Church. As a priest serving in the United States from 1908 until the 1920's he was a loud voice calling for a united American Orthodox Church and for the liturgical use of English.

While he was elected bishop of the Albanian Orthodox Church in America in 1919, the Albanian political climate (the Balkan Wars and the independence of Albania) prevented his consecration until 1923. To represent his nation, Met. Theophan served in the Albanian Parliment, and was Prime Minister of Albania in 1924. He was forced to leave Albania that same year but was unable to re-enter the United States until 1932. Met. Theophan participated in the consecration of additional bishops, which, when combined with those consecrated by Abp. Aftimios, establish the apostolic succession for many of the small Orthodox jurisdictions found in the United States.

Conclusion

These men, and others like them, sacrificed much, gave their entire adult lives to the concept of an autocephalous Catholic Church, and were the target of intense hostility by much larger institutions who, with influence and money, sought to crush these individuals and their efforts. They were all learned, well-educated men, articulate and keen. To be sure, these men were not perfect, did not always select the best candidates for ordination, and, due to the sheer loneliness, pain, frustration and sense of abandonment, reconciled themselves to the Roman Catholic Church, were received with their Episcopal status recognized, but did so as beaten men. But for these men, and the others like them who followed those lonely footsteps, Old Catholics would not exist. It is a matter of fact that many wish Old Catholics did not exist, and to this day respond with antipathy and hostility, instead of the love and grace that Christ Himself taught us.

Perhaps these men will come to be known as saints to the church they established, and, as Mar Julius I, Metropolitan of the Independent Catholic Church of Ceylon, Goa and India was, be taken from their current resting place and given a place of honor in the Cathedrals of the Church.[8] A saint is not a perfect individual, but an individual who trusts God implicitly and walks in faith, into adversity and derision for the sake of the Kingdom of God.

The Torch Is Passed

The seeds having been planted, Old Catholicism of a different type and kind, began to spread across America due to the efforts of Bishop Vilatte, Bishop de Landes Berghes and the other first generation bishops. A new generation stepped up to the plate and continued the work of their predecessors. These men benefited from the groundwork laid and were able to establish not only parishes, but dioceses and complete organizations. Many of these men knew one another and worked together. The Old Catholic Churches of the Americas emanate from their efforts. Easily, the church history of each of these individuals can constitute a book. Below is a very brief abstract of each. These men are a few of the notable second generation bishops.

Frederick E. Lloyd

Frederick Lloyd was a priest in the Anglican Church in Newfoundland, and was admitted into membership of the American Catholic Church under Archbishop Vilatte in 1912. He became rector of St. David's in Chicago, Illinois, and several years later was consecrated a bishop by Archbishop Vilatte, assisted by Bishop Miraglia-Gullotti, on December 29, 1915 and appointed coadjutor. He went on to succeed Archbishop Vilatte as the head of the American Catholic Church.

Carmel Henry Carfora

Henry Carfora was a Roman Catholic Franciscan priest, ordained in 1901, and a native of Italy. He was educated and a graduate in Philosophy and Theology from the University of Napoli, and sent to the United States to minister to the Italian Communities of New York and West Virginia. He resigned his position with the Franciscan Order and passed under the jurisdiction of Archbishop Vilatte. His great mentor while with the American Catholic Church was Bishop

Paulo Miraglia-Gullotti, bishop of the Italian contingency of the church under Archbishop Vilatte. Some historians state that Carfora was consecrated a bishop under Archbishop Vilatte by Bishop Paulo Miraglia-Gullotti. [9] After the death of his mentor, he became affiliated with Bishop Rudolph de Landas Berghes, who conditionally consecrated him on October 4th 1916. Bishop Carfora eventually succeeded Bishop Rudolph de Landas Berghes, as the Primate of the North American Old Roman Catholic Church in 1919. [10]

Francis Xavier Resch

Francis Resch was a graduate of Southern Normal University in Huntington, Tennessee and received his degree in languages. He taught Latin and German in the public high school at Earlsboro, Oklahoma in 1912. He was superintendent of schools at Leadville, Arkansas from 1930 to 1962 later moving to Kansas City, Missouri where he qualified for the priesthood under Bishop Paul Francis Cope of the Old Catholic Church of America who ordained him March 5, 1939. [11]

For a time, Fr. Resch was affiliated with Carmel Henry Carfora and the North American Old Roman Catholic Church. Henry Carfora consecrated Francis Resch Bishop on December 8, 1940. Bishop Resch later renewed his affiliation with Bishop Cope, who appointed him coadjutor with the right of succession. Bishop Resch succeeded Bishop Cope as Archbishop of the Old Catholic Church of America. [12]

George A. McGuire

George McGuire was a medical doctor, born in the West Indies. He was originally a priest in the Anglican Church, and founded of the African Orthodox Church. He was consecrated a bishop by Archbishop Vilatte on September 28th, 1921. The African Orthodox Church grew, and spread across the United States and Canada, and also established parishes in Cuba, Trinidad and South Africa. The consecration of Bishop McGuire was the last Episcopal act of Archbishop Vilatte in America. [13]

William Henry Francis Brothers

William Brothers came to America as a young lad from England. He was baptized a Roman Catholic. The family settled in Waukegan, Illinois, an industrial city between Chicago and Milwaukee. He heard the call to the cloister at an early age and although there were several Benedictine monasteries within one hundred miles of Waukegan, he chose not to enter either. At some time in his early life he became associated with the Episcopal Church and the Oxford Movement.

Brothers decided to form his own monastic community at Waukegan. He was influenced by Dom Augustine de Angelis, OSB, former Roman Catholic Benedictine. In early 1909, the American Congregation of the Order of Saint Benedict had moved from Waukegan, Illinois to Fond du Lac, Wisconsin under the protection of Bishop Charles Grafton. He was consecrated by Prince-Bishop de Landas Berghes who eventually took up residence at Saint Dunstan Abbey. The consecration took place on October 3, 1916. After his Episcopal Consecration then Bishop Brothers made effort to unite the various Old Catholic congregations in the Central and Eastern States into one ecclesiastical body. [14]

Edward Rufane Donkin

Edward Donkin was ordained a deacon and a priest by Bishop Joseph Vilatte, and served parishes in the American Catholic Church. Later he became acquainted with Roman Catholic Bishop Eduardo Sanchez y Camacho from Mexico. Bishop Camacho was dissatisfied with the Roman Catholic hierarchy in Mexico and eventually left the Roman Catholic Church to establish a Mexican National Catholic Church. Edward Donkin was consecrated a bishop by Bishop Camacho. Bishop Donkin continued to be active in the Old Catholic Movement.

Carlos Duarte Costa

Bishop Costa was a Roman Catholic Bishop in Brazil, who objected to what he perceived as the local Roman Catholic Church's poor treatment of the country's indigent. He left the Roman Catholic Church to establish the Catholic Apostolic Church of Brazil. His apostolic lines joined the traditional Old Catholic and Oriental apostolic lines of succession of Arnold Matthew and Joseph Vilatte, and are part of many Old Catholic Churches in the Americas today.

ENDNOTES FOR CHAPTER TWO

[1.] Claude B. Moss, *The Old Catholic Movement*, Third Printing (SPCK, London, 1977) p. 278

[2.] Ibid, p. 278-279.

[3.] Instrument of Episcopal Consecration of Archbishop Vilatte, signed by Mar Julius I.

[4.] The Archives of the American Congregation of St. Benedict, Bishop Donald Pierce Weeks, OSB, Abbot-Ordinary. 2002, 2003. Used by permission, 2003.

[5.] The Archives of the American Congregation of St. Benedict, Bishop Donald Pierce Weeks, OSB, Abbot-Ordinary. 2002, 2003. Used by permission, 2003.

[6.] Historical Vignettes from the Old Catholic Church of America, Archbishop-Metropolitan James Bostwick, 2003. Used by permission, 2003.

[7.] Ibid.

[8.] Courtesy of the Malankaran Syriac Orthodox Church.

[9.] Historical Vignettes from the Old Catholic Church of America, Archbishop-Metropolitan James Bostwick, 2003. Used by permission, 2003.

[10.] Ibid.

[11.] Ibid.

[12.] Ibid.

[13.] African Orthodox Church Records, RG 005, *Historical Note*, Archives and Manuscripts Dept., Pitt Theology Library, Emory University. Used by Permission, 2003.

[14.] The Archives of the American Congregation of St. Benedict, Bishop Donald Pierce Weeks, OSB, Abbot-Ordinary. Used by permission, 2003.

3

Catechetical Expression of Old Catholic Faith in the Americas

Our catechetical instruction in the Faith is drawn from the instructive teachings of both Archbishop Vilatte and Archbishop Matthew, which form the frame around which the following instruction is provided, along with other informative sources. Old Catholicism in the United States is both Eastern and Western in nature. Even as Old Catholicism made its way to the Americas, Eastern Orthodoxy and the Oriental Orthodox Churches were called to play a part. Unlike our European Utrecht Union counterparts, Old Catholicism in the United States remained staunchly sacramental in nature and infused Eastern Orthodox expressions of Faith and understanding that make it unique and different from its counterparts.

In order to understand the foundational teachings of American Old Catholicism, we must look at the catechetical expressions of faith of these individuals. We will look at each statement and expression, and then the synthesis with Orthodox theological expression.

Bishop Mathew's Act of Union of 1911[1]

Bishop Arnold Mathew severed relations with the Utrecht Union. Looking for recognition from a major catholic-orthodox body, he petitioned and was received into the Syrian Orthodox Communion under Patriarch Meletios of Antioch in 1911. The "Statement of Faith" that follows is the declaration Bishop Mathew submitted as part of his petition.

Statement of Faith submitted by Bishop Arnold Mathew

1. The Way of Salvation. Eternal Salvation is promised to mankind only through the merits of our Savior Jesus Christ, and upon condition of obedience to the teaching of the Gospel, which requires Faith, Hope, and Charity, and the due observance of the ordinances of the Orthodox and Catholic religion.

2. Faith, Hope and Charity. Faith is a virtue infused by God, whereby man accepts, and believes without doubting, whatever God has revealed in the Church concerning true religion.

Hope is a virtue infused by God, and following upon Faith; by it man puts his entire trust and confidence in the goodness and mercy of God, through Jesus Christ, and looks for the fulfillment of the Divine promises made to those who obey the Gospel.

Charity is a virtue infused by God, and likewise consequent upon Faith, whereby man, loving God above all things for His own sake, and his neighbor as himself for God's sake, yields up his will to a joyful obedience to the revealed will of God in the Church.

3. The Church. God has established the Holy Catholic Church upon earth to be the pillar and ground of the revealed Truth; and has committed to her the guardianship of the Holy Scriptures and of Holy Tradition, and the power of binding and loosing.

4. The Creed. The Catholic Church has set forth the principle doctrines of the Christian Faith in 12 articles of the Creed, as follows:

I believe in One God, the Father, The Almighty, maker of the heaven and earth, and all that is seen and unseen.

I believe in one Lord Jesus Christ, the only begotten Son of God, begotten of the Father before all worlds, God from God, Light from Light, true God from true God, begotten not made, of one substance with the Father. Through Him all things were made. For us and for our salvation he came down from heaven, by the power of the Holy Spirit he was born of the Virgin Mary, and became man. For our sake he was crucified under Pontius Pilate, he suffered died and was buried. On the third day he rose again in the fulfillment of scriptures, he ascended into heaven and is seated at the right hand of the Father. He will come again in glory to judge the living and the dead, and his Kingdom will have no end.

I believe in the Holy Spirit, the Lord and Giver of Life, who proceeds from the Father, who together with the Father and the Son the Spirit is worshipped and glorified, and has spoken through the prophets. I believe in one Holy Catholic and Apostolic church. I acknowledge one baptism for the remission of sins, I look for the resurrection of the dead and the life of the world to come. Amen.

This sacred Creed is sufficient for the establishment of the Truth, inasmuch as it explicitly teaches the perfect doctrine of the Father, the Son, and the Holy Ghost.

5. The Sacraments. The fundamental ordinances of the Gospel, instituted by Jesus Christ as a special means of conveying Divine grace and influence to the souls of men, which are commonly called Mysteries or Sacraments, are seven in number, namely, Baptism, Confirmation (Chrismation), the Holy Eucharist, Holy Orders, Matrimony, Penance, and Unction.

Baptism is the first Sacrament of the Gospel, administered by three-fold immersion in or affusion with water, with the words, "I baptize thee in the name of the Father, and of the Son, and of the Holy Ghost." It admits the recipient into the Church, bestows upon him the forgiveness of sins, original and actual, through the Blood of Christ, and causes in him a spiritual change called Regeneration. Without valid Baptism no other Sacrament can be validly received.

Confirmation, or Chrismation, is a Sacrament in which the baptized person, on being anointed with Sacred Chrism consecrated by the Bishops of the Church, with the imposition of hands, receives the sevenfold gifts of the Holy Ghost to strengthen him in the grace which he received at Baptism, making him a strong and perfect Christian and a good soldier of Christ.

The Holy Eucharist is a Sacrament in which, under the appearances of bread and wine, the real and actual Body and Blood of Christ are given and received for the remission of sins, the increase of Divine grace, and the reward of everlasting life. After the prayer of Invocation of the Holy Ghost in the Liturgy, the bread and wine are entirely converted into the living Body and Blood of Christ by an actual change of being, to which the philosophical terms of Transubstantiation and Transmutation are rightly applied. The celebration of this Mystery or Sacrament, commonly called the Mass, constitutes the chief act of Christian worship, being a sacrificial Memorial or re-Presentation of our Lord's death. It is not a repetition of the Sacrifice offered once for all upon Calvary, but is a perpetuation of that Sacrifice by the Church on earth, as our Lord also perpetually offers it in heaven. It is a true and propitiatory Sacrifice, which is offered alike for the living and for the dead.

Holy Order is a Sacrament in which the Holy Ghost, through the laying-on of hands of the Bishops, consecrates and ordains the pastors and ministers of the Church, and imparts to them special grace to administer the Sacraments, to forgive sins, and to feed the flock of Christ.

Matrimony is a Sacrament in which the voluntary union of husband and wife is sanctified to become an image of the union of Christ and His Church; and grace is imparted to them to fulfill the duties of their estate and its great responsibilities, both to each other and to their children.

Penance is a Sacrament in which the Holy Ghost bestows the forgiveness of sins, by the ministry of the Priest, upon those who, having sinned after Baptism, confess their sins with true repentance; and grace is given to amend their lives thereafter.

Unction is a Sacrament in which the Priests of the Church anoint the sick with oil, for the healing of the infirmities of their souls, and if it should please God those of their bodies also.

The efficacy of the Sacraments depends upon the promise and appointment of God; howbeit they benefit only those who receive them worthily with faith, and with due preparation and disposition of mind.

6. Holy Scripture. The Scriptures are writings inspired by God, and given to the Church for her instruction and edification. The Church is therefore the custodian and the only Divinely appointed interpreter of Holy Scripture.

7. Tradition. The Apostolic and Ecclesiastical Traditions received from the seven General Councils and the early Fathers of the Church may not be rejected, but are to be received and obeyed as being both agreeable to Holy Scripture and to that Authority with which Christ endowed His Church. Matters of discipline and ceremonial do not rank on the same level with matters of Faith or Morals, but may be altered from time to time and from place to place by the Authority of the Church, according as the welfare and greater devotion of the faithful may be furthered thereby.

8. The Communion of Saints. There is a Communion of Saints in the Providence of God, wherein the souls of the righteous of all ages are united with Christ in the bond of faith and love. Wherefore it is pleasing to God, and profitable to humanity, to honor the Saints and to invoke them in prayer; and also to pray for the faithful departed.

9. Religious Symbols. The Relics and representations of Saints are worthy of honor, as are also all other religious emblems; that our minds may be encouraged to devotion and to imitation of the deeds of the just. Honor shown to such objects is purely relative, and in no way implies a confusion of the symbol with the thing signified.

10. Rites and Ceremonies. It is the duty of all Christians to join in the worship of the Church, especially in the Holy Sacrifice of the Mass, in accordance with our Lord's express command; and to conform to the ceremonies prescribed by Holy Tradition for the greater dignity of that Sacrifice and for the edification of the faithful.

11. The Moral Law. All Christians are bound to observe the Moral Law contained in the Ten Commandments of the Old Testament, developed with greater strictness in the New, founded upon the law of nature and charity, and defining our duty to God and to man. The laws of the Church are also to be obeyed, as proceeding from that Authority which Christ has committed to her for the instruction and salvation of His people.

12. The Monastic Estate. The monastic life, duly regulated according to the laws of the Church, is a salutary institution in strict accord with the Holy Scriptures; and is fully of profit to them who, after being carefully tried and examined, make full proof of their calling thereto.

ORGANIC ARTICLES

1. Head of the Church. The Foundation, Head and Supreme Pastor and Bishop of the Church is our Lord Jesus Christ Himself, from whom all Bishops and Pastors derive their spiritual powers and jurisdiction.

2. Obedience. By the law and institution of our Lord Jesus Christ in the Gospel, all Christians owe obedience and submission in spiritual things to them who have rule and authority within the Church.

3. Ministerial Authority. Our Lord Jesus Christ did not commit rule and authority within the Church to all the faithful indiscriminately, but only to the Apostles and to their lawful successors in due order.

4. Apostolic Succession. The only lawful successors of the Apostles are the Orthodox and Catholic Bishops, united by profession of the self-same belief, participation in the same Sacraments, and mutual recognition and intercommunion. The Bishops of the Church, being true successors of the Apostles, are by Divine right and appointment the rulers of the Church.

In virtue of this appointment, each individual Bishop is supreme and independent in that part of the Church which has been committed to his care, so long as he remains in Faith and Communion with the united company of Catholic Bishops, who cannot exclude any from the Church save only them who stray from the path of virtue or err in Faith.

By virtue of this same Divine appointment, the supreme Authority over the whole Church on earth belongs to the collective Orthodox and Catholic Episcopate. They alone form the highest tribunal in spiritual matters, from whose united judgment there can be no appeal; so that it is unlawful for any single Bishop, or any smaller group of Bishops apart from them, or for any secular power or state, to usurp this Authority, or for any individual Christian to substitute his own private judgment for that interpretation of Scripture or Authority which is approved by the Church.

5. Church Authority. The collective body of the Orthodox Catholic Episcopate, united by profession of the Faith, by the Sacraments, and by mutual recognition and actual intercommunion, is the source and depository of all order, authority and jurisdiction in the Church, and is the center of visible Catholic unity; so that no Pope, Patriarch or Bishop, or any number of Bishops separated from this united body can possess any authority or jurisdiction whatsoever. The authority of this collective body is equally binding, however it may be expressed: whether by a General Council or by the regular and ordinary consultation and agreement of the Bishops them-selves. It is an act of schism to appeal from the known judgment of the Orthodox and Catholic Episcopate, however it may have been ascertained; or to appeal from any dogmatic decree of any General Council even though such appeal be to a future Council. For the Episcopate, being a continuation of the Apostolate, is clearly a Divine institution, and its authority is founded in Divine right. But General councils are not of themselves of direct Divine

appointment; and so the Episcopate having clearly the Scriptural promise of Divine guidance into all Truth, cannot be hampered in the exercise of its authority by the necessity of assembling a General Council, which may obviously be rendered impossible through natural circumstances.

There have been seven General Councils only, which are recognized by the whole of Catholic Christendom, held respectively in Nicea (A.D. 325), Constantinople (381), Ephesus (431), Chalcedon (451), Constantinople (553), Constantinople (680), and Nicea (787).

At no other Councils was the entire body of the Orthodox and Catholic Episcopate representatively assembled; and the decrees and pronouncements of no others must of themselves be accepted as binding upon the consciences of the faithful.

The Authority of the Church can never be in abeyance, even though a General Council cannot be assembled. It is equally to be submitted to and obeyed in whatever way it may be exercised, and although it may be exercised only through the ordinary administration of their respective jurisdictions by individual Bishops.

6. Hierarchy. All Patriarchs, Archbishops and Metropolitans (that is to say, all Bishops exercising authority over other Bishops) owe that authority solely to the appointment or general consent of the Orthodox and Catholic Episcopate; nor can they ever cease from owing obedience to the collective body of the Episcopate in all matters concerning Faith and Morals.

7. The Five Patriarchates. There are five Patriarchates, which ought to be united and form the supreme authority in the administration of the Holy Catholic Church. These are Jerusalem, Antioch, Rome, Alexandria, and Constantinople. Unfortunately, owing to disputes and differences on the one hand and to the lust for power on the other, the Patriarchs are not at present in Communion; and the welfare of Christendom is jeopardized by their disedifying quarrels, which we pray may soon have an end.

(NB—Other partriarchates have been legally erected in addition to these.)

A Sketch of the Belief of Old Catholics [2]
by The Most Reverend Joseph Rene Vilatte

Holy Scripture:

Old Catholics receive the Holy Scriptures as God's inspired Word. This precious revelation is accepted in the sense intended by the Holy Ghost, and is interpreted by the Church, to whom it pertains to judge of the true sense and the true interpretation of the Bible. They never understand or interpret the oracles of God except in accounts with the unanimous sentiments of the Fathers. Those books are read as canonical which are generally received by the Catholic Churches throughout the world. The bishops and priests of this Church have the duty and privilege of reading the Word of God upon all the faithful. In truth they do not reecho the words of Saint Boniface, when he said "Cast aside whatever may hinder you from studying the Holy Scriptures, seek therein the divine wisdom which is brighter then gold, purer then silver, more sparkling then diamonds, clearer then crystal, more precious then topaz, the young cannot seek a better guide, and the aged cannot possess a more precious book then the Holy Scripture, which directs the vessel of our soul, and brings it without shipwreck to the blessed shores of paradise, even to the of joys divine where the angels dwell.

Creeds:

We heartily believe and receive the three symbols of the Apostles Creed, the Nicene Creed and the Creed of Athanasius; for they are consonant with the teachings of the Fathers and the testimony of the Holy Scripture.

The Councils:

We accept the seven councils recognized by all Catholic Churches, namely:

First Council of Nicaea	AD 325	against Arianism
Second Council of Contantinople	AD 381	against Appolinares/Macedonians
Third Council of Ephesus	AD 431	against Nestorianism
Fourth Council of Calcedon	AD 451	against Monophysites
Fifth Council of Constantinople	AD 553	against Nestorianism/Monophysites

| Sixth Council of Constantinople | AD 680 | against Monothelites |
| Seventh Council of Nicaea | AD 787 | against Iconoclastes |

The Sacraments:

We believe that the Sacraments of the 'New Dispensation' are not merely sacred signs which represent grace to us, nor the seals which confirm it in us, but that they are the instruments of the Holy Ghost which apply and confer grace upon us in virtue of the words pronounced and the act performed upon us from without, provided we do not raise any obstacle by our own bad dispositions.

Baptism:

We acknowledge Baptism as the Sacrament established by Christ to cleanse men from original sin, and to make them Christians. It is the Sacrament of the new birth, "Verily, verily, I say unto thee, unless a man is born again of water and the Holy Ghost, he cannot enter the Kingdom of Heaven".

Confirmation:

We believe that the Bishop is the ordinary minister of Confirmation and that in this Sacrament, the Holy Ghost is given with the fullness of His gifts. "For they had only been baptized in the Name of the Lord Jesus, then the Apostles laid their hands upon them and they received the Holy Ghost".

Penance:

We believe that it has pleased Jesus Christ to give His Church the authority to pardon those who have broken the law of the Gospel after Baptism and that every priest validly ordained has this power through the merits and in the person of Christ. "Whosoever sins you shall forgive, they are forgiven them, and whosoever sins you shall retain, they are retained".

Eucharist:

We profess that the Eucharist is both a sacrifice and a Sacrament. That is the unbloody sacrifice of the Mass, which is the central rite and most essential act of public worship a Christian owes to God, there is a true, proper, propitiatory sacrifice for the living and the dead. We maintain that the Liturgy ought to be said in the tongue understood by the people to be in accordance with the Word of God and the custom of the primitive Church. We believe in the Most Holy Sacrament of the Eucharist there is truly and really the Body and Blood of Jesus Christ. We affirm that the cup of the Lord is not to be denied to the laity; for both the parts of the Lord's Sacrament by Christ's ordinance and commandment ought to be administered to all men alike. "Verily, verily, I say unto you, except ye eat of the flesh of the Son of man, and drink His Blood, ye have no life in you".

Extreme Unction:

We believe Extreme Unction to be a Sacrament of the New Dispensation, instituted for the spiritual and corporal solace of the sick. Its efficacy and mode of administration are plainly indicated in the Catholic Epistle of Saint James. "Is any sick among you, let him bring in the priests of the Church and let them pray over him, anointing him with oil in the Name of the Lord".

Sacred Orders:

We believe that Orders is a Sacrament which confers upon those who validly receive it the power to exercise the several functions of the ministry. Bishops are the ministers of this Sacrament. The Catholic Church makes a distinction between the Minor Orders and the greater or Holy Orders; the latter being so called by reason of eminent dignity they confer and the grave obligations they impose.

Matrimony:

We believe that Holy Matrimony is a sacrament which sanctifies the lawful union of a Christian man and women. "For this reason a man shall leave his father and his mother, and shall cleave to his wife, and the two shall become one flesh. This is a great sacrament, but I speak in Christ and in His Church".

{Note of Archbishop Vilatte: None of our priests has the right to contract marriage after his ordination. But a married man having a vocation for the sacred ministry may receive holy orders notwithstanding his previous marriage contract, in accordance with the discipline which dates from the earliest ages of the faith, and is still in rigor in all the Oriental Churches}

The Church:

The visible Church of Christ is a society in which all the faithful are joined together by the profession of the same faith, and forming a body of which Jesus Christ is the Head and Source of all authority.

The Episcopate:

We believe that the Episcopate is as necessary for the life of the church, as breath is for the life of man; and that it is the common center of unity and the guardian of the deposit of divine revelation; that bishops are equal in power and authority by divine right, and that to them belongs the duty of defending the truth of Catholic tradition; to the end that, the whole church being united under their guidance, there may ever be: "O Lord, One Faith, One Baptism, One God the Father of all, who is above all, over all and in us all" Saint Paul to the Ephesians.

Monastic Life:

Old Catholics recognize that religious orders are a source of strength and benediction not to be neglected, but to be cherished and developed among the Children of God. The life of sacrifice and of super-imminent love towards God and man which characterized the Apostles, ought to be initiated by elect souls in the Church, chosen by the Holy Ghost, for a free will immolation of self of one upon the altar of charity, so that thus the example of Evangelical virtues may be offered to the world. We believe therefore that voluntary celibacy is most agreeable to God, to which many are called for the glory of God, their own souls' surer salvation, and the solace of the sick and poor. "For he who is unmarried careth for the things of the Lord; he seeketh how he may please God; but he who is married busieth himself with the affairs of the world, he seeketh how he may please his wife, and is divided". Paul to the Corinthians.

Sacred Images:

We emphatically deny the accusations of our separated brethren who pretend that Catholics adore the images of Christ, The Blessed Virgin and the Saints. We venerate them as sacred things, and representing sacred persons. The Catholic Church compels no one to use sacred images or pictures in his worship. It is recommended as a pious practice, but it is neither necessary for justification nor for salvation. We furthermore believe that when it is practiced, it should be done wisely according the spirit and rules of the Universal Church, in or. the abuses which are always so easy and hurtful in this matter.

The Saints:

We believe that there is but "One Mediator (of redemption) between God and man, to wit: The Man Christ Jesus" 1 Timothy 2-5. But that it is a good and useful thing to invoke the saints, who are our glorified brethren, in order that they may help us by their prayers; for if "for if the prayers of a righteous man availeth much" on this earth, how much more powerful must they not be when near the throne of God in the realms of glory. That our departed brethren pray for us we know from the universal tradition of the Church and from Holy Writ. As an example we find the Prophet Jeremias interceding for the people long after his death. "This is the lover of his brethren and the people of Israel; this is he who prayeth much for the people, and the entire holy nation, even Jeremias, the Prophet of God." II Mach.

Our Bond of Union:

We allow no dissidence in matters of faith, as already said we recognize the Seven Ecumenical Councils and the fountainhead for the unity of the faith. In them are the ways of peace, from them flow the stream of grace, which one day shall efface all divisions. Their kindly light shall lead all sects to unity by sincere return to Old Catholicism. Should any member of our Church unhappily rebel against the faith he would cease to be a member, and would be regard as a heathen and publican. For no one has the right to add to, or take away from, the defined faith.

<u>ENDNOTES FOR CHAPTER THREE</u>

[1.] Arnold Matthew, *Bishop Mathew's Act of Union*, (1911)

[2.] Joseph Rene Vilatte, *A Sketch of the Belief of Old Catholics,* {Translated by the J.R. Vilatte Library, The American Congregation of Saint Benedict and Saint Patrick Abbey, Oakland, CA}, Used by Permission, 2003.

4

The Synthesis And Creation of A Symbolon Of Both Eastern Orthodox and Western Latin Faith

The faith of the Old Catholic Church is, indeed, a Catholic faith. The very word "Catholic" comes from the Greek and means "universal". The Catholic faith is the universal faith, held and agreed to by the entire church, Eastern Orthodox, Oriental and Western Latin. The word "Catholic" is not a denominational name, as some would believe, but an adjective to describe the both the scope and calling of the Church of Christ. This universal faith, is held and believed by the entire church, through all her branches that have maintained Apostolic Succession and faithful adherence to the Sacraments, the Magisterium of the Church, and the Faith in Holy Scripture and Sacred Tradition. As we combine these Statements of Faith into one Symbolon, we also infuse the Eastern Orthodox and Oriental expressions of faith and understanding into it, anchored to fundamental Catholic theology, as it existed prior to the Council of Trent, and Vatican Councils I & II.

The Symbolon

1. We believe Sacred Scripture as interpreted by the Church, together with the Seven Undisputed General Councils of the Whole Church, together with doctrines believed by the Church as a whole prior to the Great Schism of 1054, as defining the belief of the Whole Church. Every person wishing to become a member of this Church must affirm this Faith as contained in the articles below.

No one symbol, creed or statement of faith, can adequately or completely identify the essence of the Almighty God, convey His greatness or provide the ultimate definitive statement. Each creed or symbol then, is a guidepost that points us in the proper direction, as we seek to grow closer to Him, as the stars guided the captains of the ships of old towards their ultimate destination, these guides point the way towards the Light, which is the true Light that enlighteneth every man.

We accept the seven councils recognized by all Catholic Churches, namely:[1]

First Council of Nicaea	AD 325	against Arianism
Second Council of Contantinople	AD 381	against Appolinares/Macedonians
Third Council of Ephesus	AD 431	against Nestorianism
Fourth Council of Calcedon	AD 451	against Monophysites
Fifth Council of Constantinople	AD 553	against Nestorianism/Monophysites
Sixth Council of Constantinople	AD 680	against Monothelites
Seventh Council of Nicaea	AD 787	against Iconoclastes

2. We affirm the Holy Scriptures of the Old and New Testaments as interpreted by the Church, as containing everything that is necessary for salvation, and as being the rule and ultimate statement of the Faith of the Church.

Holy Scripture is to be taught and interpreted by the Church, under the instruction and guidance of the Bishops of the Church. Scripture itself affirms this: "First of all you must understand this, that no prophecy of scripture is a matter of one's own interpretation, because no prophesy ever came by the impulse of man, but men moved by the Holy Spirit spoke from God." (2 Pet. 1:20-21) The teaching authority of the church is a living breathing entity, and the Sacred Tradition, which complements and not replaces Holy Scripture, provides the understanding of the Church throughout nearly two thousand years. Any interpretation or teaching as to the meaning of Sacred Scripture that is made separate from the Deposit of Faith, is then suspect.

3. We accept the Canon of Scripture as handed down from of Old.

4. We affirm the Nicene Creed as the principal creed of the Faith of the Church. We also recognize the Western Baptismal Creed, commonly called the "Apostles Creed," and the hymn commonly called the "Athanasian Creed" as representing statements of the Nicene Faith.

Nicene Creed

I believe in one God, the Father Almighty, maker of heaven and earth, and of all things visible and invisible. And in one Lord, Jesus Christ, the only begotten Son of God, and born of the Father before all ages; God of God, light of light; true God of true God; begotten, not made; consubstantial to the Father, by whom all things were made. Who for us men, and for our salvation, came down from heaven and became incarnate by the Holy Ghost, of the Virgin Mary; AND WAS MADE MAN. He was crucified also for us, suffered under Pontius Pilate, and was buried. And the third day he rose again according to the Scriptures; and ascended into heaven, sitteth at the right hand of the Father; and He is to come again with glory, to judge both the living and the dead; of whose kingdom there shall be no end. And in the Holy Ghost, the Lord and giver of life, who proceedeth from the Father; who together with the Father and the Son, is adored and glorified; who spoke by the Prophets. And in one holy Catholic and Apostolic Church. I confess one Baptism for the remission of sins. And I expect the resurrection of the dead, and the life of the world to come. Amen.

The Apostles Creed

I believe in God the Father Almighty, Maker of heaven and earth.

And in Jesus Christ his only Son our Lord; who was conceived by the Holy Ghost, born of the Virgin Mary, suffered under Pontius Pilate, was crucified, dead, and buried; he descended into hell; the third day he rose again from the dead; he ascended into heaven, and sitteth on the right hand of God the Father Almighty; from thence he shall come to judge the quick and the dead.

I believe in the Holy Ghost; the holy catholic Church; the communion of saints; the forgiveness of sins; the resurrection of the body; and the life everlasting. AMEN.

Athanasian Creed

(Marquess of Bute's English translation)

Whosoever will be saved, before all things it is necessary that he hold the Catholic Faith. Which Faith except everyone do keep whole and undefiled, without doubt he shall perish everlastingly. And the Catholic Faith is this, that we worship one God in Trinity and Trinity in Unity. Neither confounding the Persons, nor dividing the Substance. For there is one Person of the Father, another of the Son, and another of the Holy Ghost. But the Godhead of the Father, of the Son and of the Holy Ghost is all One, the Glory Equal, the Majesty Co-Eternal. Such as the Father is, such is the Son, and such is the Holy Ghost. The Father Uncreate, the Son Uncreate, and the Holy Ghost

Uncreate. The Father Incomprehensible, the Son Incomprehensible, and the Holy Ghost Incomprehensible. The Father Eternal, the Son Eternal, and the Holy Ghost Eternal and yet they are not Three Eternals but One Eternal. As also there are not Three Uncreated, nor Three Incomprehensibles, but One Uncreated, and One Uncomprehensible. So likewise the Father is Almighty, the Son Almighty, and the Holy Ghost Almighty. And yet they are not Three Almighties but One Almighty.

So the Father is God, the Son is God, and the Holy Ghost is God. And yet they are not Three Gods, but One God. So likewise the Father is Lord, the Son Lord, and the Holy Ghost Lord. And yet not Three Lords but One Lord. For, like as we are compelled by the Christian verity to acknowledge every Person by Himself to be God and Lord, so are we forbidden by the Catholic Religion to say, there be Three Gods or Three Lords. The Father is made of none, neither created, nor begotten. The Son is of the Father alone; not made, nor created, but begotten. The Holy Ghost is of the Father, and of the Son neither made, nor created, nor begotten, but proceeding.

So there is One Father, not Three Fathers; one Son, not Three Sons; One Holy Ghost, not Three Holy Ghosts. And in this Trinity none is afore or after Other, None is greater or less than Another, but the whole Three Persons are Co-eternal together, and Co-equal. So that in all things, as is aforesaid, the Unity is Trinity, and the Trinity is Unity is to be worshipped. He therefore that will be saved, must thus think of the Trinity.

Furthermore, it is necessary to everlasting Salvation, that he also believe rightly the Incarnation of our Lord Jesus Christ. For the right Faith is, that we believe and confess, that our Lord Jesus Christ, the Son of God, is God and Man.

God, of the substance of the Father, begotten before the worlds; and Man, of the substance of His mother, born into the world. Perfect God and Perfect Man, of a reasonable Soul and human Flesh subsisting. Equal to the Father as touching His Godhead, and inferior to the Father as touching His Manhood. Who, although He be God and Man, yet He is not two, but One Christ. One, not by conversion of the Godhead into Flesh, but by taking of the Manhood into God. One altogether, not by confusion of substance, but by Unity of Person. For as the reasonable soul and flesh is one Man, so God and Man is one Christ. Who suffered for our salvation, descended into Hell, rose again the third day from the dead. He ascended into Heaven, He sitteth on the right hand of the Father, God Almighty, from whence he shall come to judge the quick and the dead. At whose coming all men shall rise again with their bodies, and shall give account for their own works. And they that have done good shall go into life everlasting, and they that have done evil into everlasting fire.

This is the Catholic Faith, which except a man believe faithfully and firmly, he cannot be saved.

5. We believe that the Nicene Creed is a literal statement of the belief of the Church and is not subject to interpretation, which dismisses as merely allegorical or merely mythological any portion thereof.

The Nicene Creed, as a tool of testimony against heresy, and also as a symbolon (symbol) of faith testifies to both natural and supernatural truths, brought about by the one true God. Alongside all of the creeds and symbols of faith of the Church, it testifies to the spiritual reality of God, His salvific work in our lives, and the promise of a future with Him if we turn to Him and confess His Truth.

6. We affirm the Seven Sacraments Baptism, Holy Eucharist, Confirmation, Holy Order, Holy Matrimony, Penance and Holy Unction administered with the unfailing use of the traditional outward and visible signs, and the form, matter, ministers and intention received of old.

"Because Jesus is *The* Sacrament which makes all sacraments possible, every sacrament finds its unity in Him. No one sacrament, therefore, can be isolated from the others, nor is each sacrament administered to perform a different "job" (i.e. baptism to erase Original Sin, confirmation to impart the Spirit, the Eucharist to communicate Christ's atonement). Each sacrament manifests Christ in his wholeness, not "pieces" of His power; each brings union in and with the one Lord" [2]

"It is for this reason that the Early Christian saw the initiatory sacraments (Baptism, Confirmation, Eucharist) as a *collective whole,* each one *standing in symphony with the others* to manifest the redemptive mystery. Thus, baptism, Confirmation and the Eucharist are *inseparable,* each disclosing the reality of Christ's saving union with us. Baptism reveals God's *union* with us through Christ, Confirmation (in the East 'chrismation') manifests God's *union* with us through the Spirit's indwelling within and among us, and the Eucharist actualizes the reality of God's *union* with us as the Body of Christ. What Christ is to us in Baptism, He is to us in Confirmation and the Eucharist. Each sacrament reveals the one and same mystery, 'Christ, in you, the hope of glory' (Col. 1:27)." [3]

"Sacraments, therefore, are not empowered objects that give private blessings to solitary individuals. In no way do they fit into an individualistic frame of reference. The mysteries reveal the *bond* we share with Christ *and* the brethren (His body)."[4]

"If one sees grace as something distinct from God Himself, or as some substance He created to save us, he is bound to misunderstand sacraments and their purpose. Grace is not a mysterious force enabling man to come to God. Grace is not something God manufactured in heaven and then sent to earth to save us. Grace *is the direct and personal communion of God with His people*, and the sacraments manifest that communion. When someone is strengthened or saved by grace, he is not strengthened or saved by 'a thing' but by a *Person*."[5]

"If the sacraments reveal and manifest the presence of God and His union with men, they must be communal. God Himself is Three Persons in communion, and His union with men is through Christ in the Church Community. A Christian's reception of the sacraments, then, is to manifest his participation both in God's Communal Life and in the divine-human Community (the Church). Hence, the sacraments cannot be given to the lone, "unconnected" individual; no sacrament can exist apart from Christ Who dwells *within* His body."[6]

The mind of the Church has been expressed through her Apostles, Bishops, Teachers and Martyrs down throughout history, who, with one voice, confidently profess the spiritual truths of the sacraments, which flow from Christ Jesus Himself.

Baptism. Baptism is the initiation of the new believer into life as a Christian. It is mandated and established by Christ Himself, and the Apostles strictly instructed every new convert that they must be baptized. Entire households were baptized, including servants, children and infants, without delay. Indeed, St. Paul answers the jailer who asks, "What must I do to be saved?" by responding that he must believe and be baptized, which he did, along with his entire household. (Acts 16:27-33)

Inherent in baptism is God's grace, His love, and a beginning for us to commune with Him through the sacramental covenant bond begun through baptism. For this reason, He commanded His Disciples to baptize, so as to initiate individuals into the Body of Christ.

(Matthew 28:18-20) "All authority in heaven and on earth has been given to me. Go therefore and make disciples of all nations, baptizing them in the name of the Father and of the Son and of the Holy Spirit, teaching them to observe all that I have commanded you; and lo, I am with you always, to the close of the age."

Baptism is not optional, nor is it a mere ceremony to demonstrate one's belief in God. Baptism is commanded by Christ Himself, a necessity for us to be able to "enter the kingdom of God."

(John 3:4-5,22) "Jesus answered him,' Truly, truly, I say to you, unless one is born anew, he cannot see the kingdom of God.' Nicodemus said to him, 'How can a man be born when he is old? Can he enter a second time into his mother's womb and be born?' Jesus answered, 'Truly, truly, I say to you, unless one is born of water and the Spirit, he cannot enter the kingdom of God. That which is born of the flesh is flesh, and that which is born of the Spirit is spirit...' After this Jesus and his disciples went into the land of Judea; there he remained with them and baptized."

Infants and children too, are to be baptized as soon as possible. (Matthew 19:13-15) "Then children were brought to him that he might lay his hands on them and pray. The disciples rebuked the people; but Jesus said, 'Let the children come to me, and do not hinder them; for to such belongs the kingdom of heaven.' And he laid his hands on them and went away."

"At dawn a prayer shall be offered over the water. Where there is no scarcity of water the stream shall flow through the baptismal font or pour into it from above; but if water is scarce, whether as constant condition or on occasion, then use whatever water is available. Let them remove their clothing. Baptise first the children; and if they can speak for themselves, let them do so. Otherwise, let the parents or other relatives speak for them." St. Hippolytus of Rome, *The Apostolic Tradition* 215 AD [7]

"The Church received from the Apostles the tradition of giving Baptism even to infants. For the Apostles, to whom were committed the secrets of divine mysteries, knew that there is in everyone the innate stain of sin, which must be washed away through water and the Spirit." Origen, *Commentaries on Romans* 244 AD [8]

"If, in the case of the worst sinners and of those who formerly sinned much against God, when afterwars they believe, the remission of their sins is granted and no one is held back from Baptism and grace, how much more, then, should an infant not be held back, who, having but recently been born, has done no sin, except that, born of flesh according to Adam, he has contracted the contagion of that old death from his first being born. For this very reason does he approach more easily to receive the remission of sins: because the sins forgiven him are not his on but those of another." St. Cyprian of Carthage, *Letter of Cyprian and his Colleagues in Council to the Number of Sixty-six: To Fidus.* 251/252 AD [9]

As circumcision was for the Jew, initiation into accountability under Mosaic Law and the Old Covenant, Baptism is the initiation into accountability as a Christian and the New Covenant. And like the requirement of circumcision of the Old Covenant, one who was born into the first-born nation of God was circumcised on the eight day (Luke 1:21) or if converting as an adult, would still undergo circumcision (Genesis 17:9-14). The law of God was absolute, and to violate it would bring God's judgment (Exodus 4:24-26). In the New Testament man receives instruction directly from God made man, in Christ Jesus, that, in order to be saved, it was necessary to repent and be baptized. Jesus instructed His disciples to "Go therefore, and make disciples of all nation, baptizing them in the name of the Father, and of the Son and of the Holy Spirit, teaching them to observe all that I have commanded you; and lo, I am with you always, to the close of the age." (Matthew 28:19-20)

Holy Eucharist.

(John 1:28-30) "…The next day he saw Jesus coming towards him, and said, 'Behold, the Lamb of God, who takes away the sin of the world."

(1 Cor. 11:25) "This is my body which is for you. Do this in remembrance of me.' In the same way also the cup, after supper, saying 'This cup is the new covenant in my blood. Do this, as often as you drink it, in remembrance of me."

Throughout both the Old and the New Testament, we see God present to His people under the appearance of various created things. We turn to Scripture and see this in Exodus 3:2-6, Exodus 13:21-22, Matthew 3:16, Genesis 18:1-2 and Matthew 13:55.

(1 Cor. 10:16) "This cup of blessing which we bless, is it not a participation in the blood of Christ? The bread that we break, is it not a participation in the body of Christ? Because there is one bread, we who are many are one body."

Christ Himself taught us that He is truly present in the consecrated Bread and Wine, and repeated this teaching several times in His ministry. When

He taught that we must eat His flesh and drink His blood, many of His followers departed. Did they misunderstand? Apparently not, a misunderstanding would not warrant leaving the company of the man they believed was the Messiah. All too clearly they understood that this was not a euphemism, but a testimony of a supernatural reality, one that they refused to accept, since their human intellect could not comprehend it. Nowhere does Jesus indicate that he meant that the bread and wine "represent" His Body and Blood, or that he was merely speaking metaphorically. The writers, teachers, bishops and leaders of the early church all speak unanimously about their belief of the Real Presence of Christ in the Eucharist.

"The most intimate link between the Eucharist and a meal is the Passover meal. This is particularly evident in the way the Old Testament Jew celebrated it as a means to remember his deliverance from Egypt....'to remember' had a distinctively different meaning to the Jew and other Eastern peoples that merely 'to recount' or 'to recall.' This is a crucial point. When Jesus asked us to perform the Eucharistic rite in 'remembrance' of Him, He obviously had the Jewish understanding of 'remember' in mind...

The word 'remembrance' in the Gospel accounts of the Lord's Supper is translated from the Greek word anamnesis. This word is difficult to translate into just one English word. When we use 'remembrance' or 'memorial' to translate it, we are often led astray from its deeper significance. These usually connote something absent-something which is only mentally recollected. However, they do not capture the Biblical sense of 'remembrance' (anamnesis).[10]

According to the Scriptures, when an event from the past is being 're-presented' before God in such a way that what is being symbolized becomes operative in the present, one 'remembers' it.[13] To remember in this sense, then is to defy the historical limitations of time. When the Jews 'remembered' the Passover, for instance, they re-lived and re-entered their exodus from Egypt once again. God's deliverance of them was again made real."[11]

"This background ties directly into our understanding of the Eucharist. When the Lord asked us to 'do this in remembrance' of Him, He was asking us to remember—'to do anamnesis'—in the same sense as the Jews 'remembered' their deliverance in the Passover Feast. He was not asking us merely to mentally recall His death on our behalf. In the Eucharistic celebration, we are to 'remember' our salvation through Christ's offering of Himself.

Through this 're-living' or 're-entering' connoted by anamnesis, each believer personally participates in the event of His once-for-all sacrifice."[12]

"In this Eucharistic remembrance—like the Jews in their Passover celebration—each is actively delivered afresh from slavery, sin and death. Anamnetically, each enters into God's salvation in the corporate celebration of the Eucharist, just as anamnetically each Jew entered into he experience of deliverance again and again at each Passover. And just as the Jews would not have said that the firstborn of Egypt were slain again and again because of this 'remembrance' of their deliverance, so neither did the Early Church say that Christ is crucified again and again through her "remembrance' of His sacrifice. The spirit-filled celebration of the Eucharist does not re-create history. It allows the Church to experience the saving effects Christ accomplished in history, effects that are now experienced and manifested in the gathered Assembly's 'remembrance." [13]

Anamnesis not only calls us to re-live (and thus to re-experience) what is being 'remembered,' it also invites us to taste the future. The Passover did this by foreshadowing the Eucharistic celebration not only in its rite, but also in the salvation which was yet to come. Passover night was the night on which the Jews had been redeemed in the past, and on which they would be redeemed in the future. 'When the Jews at the first Passover remembered their deliverance, they also 'remembered-anticipated' their ultimate deliverance in the One Who was to come.' The Eucharist is a celebration of the Pascal mystery now completed in Christ…"

"…Christ Jesus is truly present in the Eucharist, body, blood, soul and divinity. The species of bread and wine continue after the prayers of consecration [and the Epiclesis], and retain their physical reality after the change of the substance."[14]

"The Body and Blood of Christ together with His Soul and His Divinity and therefore the Whole Christ are truly present in the Eucharist."[15] We find testimony to this again and again in the Bible, as well as throughout nearly two thousand years of Christianity.

We see that Christ is both High Priest, and Perfect Sacrifice: "So also Christ did not exalt himself to be made a high priest, but was appointed by him who said to him, 'Thou are a priest for ever, after the order of Mel-chiz-e-dek." (Heb 5:5-6)

"I have no taste for corruptible food nor for the pleasures of this life. I desire the Bread of God, which is the Flesh of Jesus Christ, who was of the seed of David; and for drink I desire His Blood, which is love incorruptible." St. Ignatius of Antioch, *Letter To The Romans* 110 A.D. [16]

"For not as common bread nor common drink do we receive these; but since Jesus Christ our Savior was made incarnate by the Word of God and had both flesh and blood for our salvation, so too, as we have been taught, the food which has been made into the Eucharist by the Eucharistic prayer set down by Him, and by the change of which our blood and flesh is nourished, is both the flesh and the blood of that incarnated Jesus." St. Justin the Martyr, *First Apology*, inter 148-155 A.D. [17]

"They are vain in every respect, who despise the entire dispensation of God, and deny the salvation of the body and spurn its regeneration, saying that it is not capable of immortality. If the body be not saved, then, in fact, neither did the Lord redeem us with His Blood; and neither is the cup of the Eucharist the partaking of His Blood nor is the Bread which we brake the partaking of His Body…As we are His members, so too are we nourished by means of created things, He Himself granting us the creation, causing His sun to rise and sending rain as He wishes. He has declared the cup, a part of creation, to be His own Blood, from which He causes our blood to flow; and the bread, a part of creation, He has established as His own Body, from which He gives increase to our bodies.

When, therefore, the mixed cup and the baked bread received the Word of God and becomes the Eucharist, the Body and Blood of Christ, and from these the substance of our flesh is increased and supported, how can they say that the flesh is not capable of receiving the gift of God, which is eternal life—flesh which is nourished by the Body and Blood of the Lord, and is in fact a member of Him?"

In this regard the blessed Paul says in his Epistles to the Ephesians: 'Because we are members of His Body, from His flesh and His bones.'" St. Irenaeus, *Against Heresies*, inter 180/199 A.D. [18]

"You know that you were ransomed from the futile ways inherited from your fathers, not with perishable things such as silver or gold, but with the precious blood of Christ, like that of a lamb without blemish or spot. He was destined before the foundation of the world but was made manifest at the end of times for your sake. (1 Pet. 1:18-20) Indeed, as Christ was being prepared for crucifixion, the sacrificial lambs of Passover were, at that very time, being prepared for slaughter as well. So He became our new Paschal sacrifice, and we were commanded to "remember" and spiritually re-enter the communal meal with Him during the Eucharist, partaking of a supernatural gift that human knowledge cannot explain and is a mystery of faith. Worthy is the Lamb that was slain!

Confirmation.

"We believe that the Bishop is the ordinary minister of Confirmation and that in this Sacrament, the Holy Ghost is given with the fullness of His gifts. 'For they had only been baptized in the Name of the Lord Jesus, then the Apostles laid their hands upon them and they received the Holy Ghost".[19]

"Confirmation, or Chrismation, is a Sacrament in which the baptized person, on being anointed with Sacred Chrism consecrated by the Bishops of the Church, with the imposition of hands, receives the sevenfold gifts of the Holy Ghost to strengthen him in the grace which he received at Baptism, making him a strong and perfect Christian and a good soldier of Christ." [20]

"Now when the apostles at Jerusalem heard that Samaria had received the Word of God, they sent to them Peter and John, who came down and prayed for them that they might receive the Holy Spirit; for it had not fallen on any of them, but they had only been baptized I the name of the Lord Jesus. Then they laid their hands on them and they received the Holy Spirit." (Acts 8:14-17)

"And to you in like manner, after you had come up from the pool of the sacred streams, there was given chrism, the antitype of that with which Christ was anointed and this is the Holy Spirit. But beware of supposing that this is ordinary ointment. For just as the Bread of the Eucharist after the invocation of the Holy Spirit is simple bread no longer, but the Body of Christ, so also this holy ointment is no longer plain ointment, nor so to speak, common, after the invocation. Rather, it is the gracious gift of Christ; and it is made fit for the imparting of His Godhead by the coming of the Holy Spirit. This ointment is symbolically applied to your forehead and other senses; and while your body is anointed with the visible ointment, your soul is sanctified by the Holy and Lifecreating Spirit." St. Cyril of Jerusalem, *Catechetical Lectures,* 350 A.D. [21]

"While Apollos was at Corinth, Paul passed through the upper country and came to Ephesus. There he found some disciples. And he said to them, 'Did you receive the Holy Spirit when you believed?' And they said, 'No, we have never even heard that there is a Holy Spirit.' And he said, 'Into what then were you baptized?' They said, 'Into John's baptism.' And Paul said, 'John baptized with the baptism of repentance, telling the people to believe in the one who was to come after him, that is, Jesus.' On hearing this, they were baptized in the name of the Lord Jesus. And when Paul had laid his hands upon them, the Holy Spirit came on them; and they spoke in tongues and prophesied." (Acts 19:1-7)

"Therefore let us leave the elementary doctrine of Christ and go on to maturity, not laying again a foundation of repentance from dead works and of faith toward God, with instruction about ablutions, the laying on of hands, the resurrection of the dead, and eternal judgment." (Heb. 6:1-2)

Holy Orders.

"We believe that Orders is a Sacrament which confers upon those who validly receive it the power to exercise the several functions of the ministry. Bishops are the ministers of this Sacrament. The Catholic Church makes a distinction between the Minor Orders and the greater or Holy Orders; the latter being so called by reason of eminent dignity they confer and the grave obligations they impose." [22]

Although not necessary for ordination, the state of celibacy in the priesthood is an honorable, sacred and altogether wholesome thing, for those men who are truly called to it. Celibacy for the sake of the Kingdom of God is biblically supported, "For there are eunuchs who have been so from birth, and there are eunuchs who have been made eunuchs by men, and there are eunuchs who have made themselves eunuchs for the sake of the kingdom of heaven. He who is able to receive this, let him receive this." (Matthew 19:12)

The appointment and selection to Holy Orders is to a supernatural and sacred office, as a priest of the New Covenant, in the shadow of the Levitical priesthood of the Old Covenant. That this is a sacred office, established by Christ, and understood as such by the Apostles is thus underscored, "For he was numbered among us, and allotted his share in this ministry. (Now this man bought a field with the reward of his wickedness; and falling headlong he burst open in the middle and all his bowels gushed out. And it became known to all the inhabitants of Jerusalem, so that the field was called in their language A-kel da-ma, that is, Field of Blood.) For it is written in the book of Psalms, 'Let his habitation become desolate, and let there be no one to live in it'; and 'His *office* let another take." (Acts 1:17-20)

Likewise, St. Paul, too, understood Apostleship to be a sacred office, established by Christ in His appointment of the Twelve, and carried on by others appointed and selected by them, through the laying on of hands and prayer:

"The saying is sure: If any one aspires to the *office* of bishop, he desires a noble task. Now a bishop must be above reproach, the husband of one wife, temperate, sensible, dignified, hospitable an apt teacher, no drunkard, not violent but gentle, not quarrelsome, and no lover of money." (1 Tim 3:1-3)

Sacramental ordination to Holy Orders takes place with the laying on of hands by a bishop and with the prayer of consecration. The importance of this act is seen throughout Scripture, and the understanding that, through the laying on of hands, a spiritual authority, originating with Christ and passed to the Disciples, is supernaturally conveyed. "Do not be hasty in the laying on of hands, nor participate in another man's sins; keep yourself pure." (1 Tim 4:22)

Every deacon and priest is tied to the bishop spiritually, as the bishop posses the fullness of the priesthood, given the Apostles by Christ Jesus Himself. Every bishop then, is spiritually bound to Christ who is the High Priest of the New Covenant. "So also Christ did not exalt himself to be made a high priest, but was appointed by him who said to him, 'Thou are a priest for ever, after the order of Mel-chiz-e-dek." (Heb 5:5-6)

Holy Matrimony.

Sacramental matrimony is only possible between a man and woman who both of the single estate and Christian, as evidenced by Trinitarian baptism. While a "natural marriage" may be possible between a Christian and a non-Christian, the same bond is not created as the non-Christian is not a believer and does not agree and belief in the sacramental covenant. However, the Christian spouse may yet bring God's blessing to the unbelieving spouse through obedience to God, fidelity in all things to the spouse, prayer and supplication. For the Christian, no marriage outside of the Church, whether to a Christian or a non-believer, is valid. A marriage contract executed by the parties, through governmental authorities, is never valid in the eyes of the Church, although a civil contract of marriage may exist. Civil government can never provide the necessary essentials for a sacramental marriage. Sacramental marriage is to be effected among the brethren of the Church, officiated by the Bishop, priest, or deacon, and in the presence of the Church as a witness.

"Matrimony is a Sacrament in which the voluntary union of husband and wife is sanctified to become an image of the union of Christ and His Church; and grace is imparted to them to fulfill the duties of their estate and its great responsibilities, both to each other and to their children."[23]

Civil divorce does not terminate a sacramental marriage, and never can. A valid marriage is indissoluble unto death of one of the spouses, releasing the other. A sacramental marriage may be found to have not been effected, due to some defect of the essential matter, for or intent of one or both of the intended parties. Should it be found that a defect did, in fact, exist, which would prevent the sacramental marriage from being bonded, then the Church, upon due examination, would issue a Declaration of Nullity. Such a declaration would have no effect upon the legitimacy of any children conceived during the cohabitation. To eliminate most problems before they occur, the Church, through the parish priest, provides pre-nuptial instruction, to ensure, as much as is possible, that both parties understand the sacramental nature of marriage.

Matrimony is the union of two lives, a man and a woman, into one. This union, for the Christian is holy and sacramental, for we invoke the holy name of God, and ask him to bless and ratify the union, entering the man and woman into a covenant agreement with God, asking His help. This brings His blessings as a result of this covenant, and His punishment for violating it. When the bonds of Matrimony are violated, the covenant promises made to God are also violated, and the violating partner sins against God.

(Matthew 19:4) "He answered, "Have you not read that he who made them male and female, and said, 'For this reason a man shall leave his father and mother and be joined to his wife, and the two shall become one'? So they are no longer two but one. What God has joined together, let no man put asunder.' They said to him, 'Why then did Moses command one to give a certificate of divorce, and to put her away?' He said to them, 'For your hardness of heart Moses allowed you to divorce your wives, but from the beginning it was not so. And I say to you: whoever divorces his wife, except for unchastity, and marries another, commits adultery; and he who marries a divorced woman, commits adultery." Matrimony was, from the beginning, meant to be a permanent state. As a covenant made between a man, a woman and God, it was, and is, a sacred, holy estate, sealed with God's covenant blessing. To break the vows of Matrimony then, necessarily means that one subjects themselves to God's punishment for breaking the covenant with the spouse and with Him.

"For I hate divorce, says the Lord the God of Israel, and covering one's garments with violence, says the Lord of Hosts. So take heed to yourselves and do not be faithless." (Mal. 2:16)

For anyone who thinks that the prohibition was abolished in the New Covenant with Christ, they would be woefully mistaken, for we read: "Everyone who divorces his wife and marries another commits adultery, and he who marries a woman divorced from her husband commit adultery." (Luke 16:18)

We also read: "Do you not know that the unrighteous will not inherit the Kingdom of God? Do not be deceived; neither the immoral, nor idolators, nor adulterers, nor homosexuals, nor thieves, nor the greedy, nor drunkards, nor revilers, nor robbers will inherit the Kingdom of God." (1 Cor. 6:9-11) Even for Christians, the life we live on this earth affects the measure of reward or judgment we shall inherit in the life to come. One cannot become part of the Body of Christ, that is to say, the Church, and not strive to live the Christ like life, but wallow rebelliously in sin, and expect reward.

Penance.

"Penance is a Sacrament in which the Holy Ghost bestows the forgiveness of sins, by the ministry of the Priest, upon those who, having sinned after Baptism, confess their sins with true repentance; and grace is given to amend their lives thereafter." [24]

Christ left us the gift of forgiveness of sins committed throughout our lives, entrusting the power to bind and loose, and to forgive or retain sins to His Disciples, who, in the sacrament of Holy Orders, passed this sacred authority on to the priests and bishops of the Church. Christ recognized our need to verbally confess, and our human need to hear Him, through the leaders of the Church, say, "In the name of Jesus Christ, your sins are forgiven you". The sacrament of penance is a hard one for many, who are too proud or embarrassed or concerned about what others will say. We must remember that "all have sinned, and fallen short of the glory of God" and so we must put our spiritual life first, and if humbled in doing so, all the better.

(Matthew 9:1-8) "And getting into a boat he crossed over and came to his own city. And behold, they brought to him a paralytic, lying on his bed; and when Jesus saw their faith he said to the paralytic, 'Take heart, my son; your sins are forgiven.' And behold, some of the scribes said to themselves, 'This man in blaspheming.' But Jesus, knowing their thoughts, said, 'Why do you think evil in your hearts? For which is easier; to say, "Your sins are forgiven," or to say, "Rise and walk"? But that you may know that the Son of man has authority on earth to forgive sins'—he said to the paralytic—'Rise, take up your bead and go home.' And he rose and went home. When the crowds saw it, they were afraid, and they glorified God, who had given such authority to men."

Scripture bears witness to Christ imparting His spiritual authority to the Disciples, to bind and loose, to forgive or retain sins. Christ Himself established the sacrament of Penance and gave His disciples the mandate to go forth and do it.

(Matthew 18:18-19) "Truly, I say to you, whatever you bind on earth shall be bound in heaven, and whatever you loose on earth shall be loosed in heaven. Again I say to you, if two of you agree on earth about anything they ask, it will be done for them by my Father in heaven."

(John 20:22) "And when he had said this, he breathed on them, and said to them, 'Received the Holy Spirit. If you forgive the sins of any, they are forgiven; if you retain the sins of any, they are retained."

Confessing our sins is necessary in our journey with Christ, and cleanses us so that we may better continue that journey, conforming our life to Him. Refusal to do penance is sinful, whether out of obstinate refusal, guilt or embarrassment. It is far more important for us to obtain God's grace through the sacrament of penance than be concerned about what other people think.

(1 John 1:8) "If we say we have no sin, we deceive ourselves, and the truth is not in us. If we confess our sins, he is faithful and just, and will forgive our sins, and cleans us from all unrighteousness."

"Therefore confess your sins to one another, and pray for one another, that you may be healed. "(James 5:16) This can be seen in the general confession of the "Confiteor" during the Sacred Mass, where we say, "I confess to Almighty God...."

Holy (Extreme) Unction.

"We believe Extreme Unction to be a Sacrament of the New Dispensation, instituted for the spiritual and corporal solace of the sick. Its efficacy and mode of administration are plainly indicated in the Catholic Epistle of Saint James. "Is any sick among you, let him bring in the priests of the Church and let them pray over him, anointing him with oil in the Name of the Lord".[25]

"Unction is a Sacrament in which the Priests of the Church anoint the sick with oil, for the healing of the infirmities of their souls, and if it should please God those of their bodies also." [26]

Holy Unction is also called "Anointing of the Sick" and has been a sacrament of the Church from its inception. Scripture bears witness to the establishment of this sacrament and the proper minister of it.

"Is any among you sick? Let him call for the elders of the church, and let them pray over him, anointing him with oil in the name of the Lord; and the prayer of faith will save the sick man, and the Lord will raise him up; and if he has committed any sins, he will be forgiven." (James 5:14-15)

The elders (bishops and priests) of the Church were (and are) the proper ministers of this sacrament, and so it continues from the beginning of Christianity to our present age. They are the successors to the Apostles, to whom Christ gave the authority to anoint and pray for the healing of the sick. "And they cast many demons, and anointed with oil many that were sick and healed them." (Mark 6:13)

7. We affirm the Historic three-fold ministry of Bishops, Priests and Deacons, and the traditional rights and powers thereof, locally adapted in the methods of its administration according to the needs of the nations in which the Church resides, but historic in form, matter, ministers and intention.

Deacon. The deacon has the ministry of service to others as an assistant to the bishop, but differently from the priest. The deacon ministers to the temporal need of the community, ensuring that all are cared for, especially the very young and very old or infirmed. Like the priest, he is ordained through the laying on of hands to his sacred office.

Priest. The priest is the assistant of the bishop, at the sacrifice of the Mass, in administering the sacraments of Baptism, Holy Matrimony, and the Anointing of the Sick. To the priest is given the spiritual authority from the bishop to consecrate the bread and wine into the Body and Blood of our Lord, during the Mass.

Bishop. The Church's bishops are the successors to the Apostles, and posses (and are posses by) the fullness of the priesthood of the New Covenant. From the bishop, the deacon and priest is spiritually linked, for it is the bishop alone who ordains those called to the diaconate and the priesthood. To the bishop is charged the spiritual welfare of the local church, its instruction, guidance and process of spiritual maturity. The bishop is the spiritual Shepherd, the Father of the local church in their faith, and is configured to Christ. Every validly ordained (consecrated) bishop stands in a line of succession, through prayer and the laying on of hands when ordained, back in time to the Apostles themselves, *and ultimately to Christ.*

Each bishop is responsible for the conduct and care of the local church under his care. "While the bond of concord remains and the indivisible sacrament of the Catholic Church continues, each bishop disposes and directs his own work as one who must give an account of his administration to the Lord." St. Cyprian of Carthage, *Letter of Cyprian to Antonias, A Bishop in Numidia* 251-252 A.D. [27]

8. We affirm that, in accordance with Sacred Scripture and ancient Tradition, only males may be ordained to the Diaconate, Priesthood, or Episcopate.

The selection of the twelve disciples is representative of the twelve tribes of Israel, being re-established, but his time in a manner that includes peoples of every nation, into this new kingdom, the Kingdom of God. As the Levitical priests offered tribute and sacrifice to God on behalf of the people, this natural symbol, which lacked supernatural grace, was perfected in the New Testament, with new priests who offer a supernatural Sacrifice which did not merely atone for sin, but cleansed us from sin, and purchased our freedom, as no Old Testament sacrifice could do. And so the supernatural reality of spiritual freedom from sin realized in the New Testament, perfects what could not have been achieved through sacrifice in the Old Covenant. The selection of the twelve was prophetic, and emphasizes that Christ replaced the natural symbols of the Old Covenant with the supernatural realities of the New Covenant, and He selected the twelve to bring to fulfillment what was pre-figured in the Old. His selection of the twelve was His choice, for His reasons, and not those of society. Likewise did the Apostles select men for ordination, and so it has been for the life of the Church.

Attempts to impute a sociopolitical concept into the faith for a perceived wrong are misguided, and demean the singular dignity of female and male alike, as each, being equal in human dignity, has certain uniqueness, given by God to each for a particular purpose. To attempt to negate or minimize these uniquenesses is to reject the gifts of God, in whatever form they take, and live in rebellion against His plan for our life.

9. We affirm the Real Presence of Our Lord in the Eucharist when the Eucharist is performed by a validly ordained Priest of the Holy Catholic Church, with the elements ordained by Christ, and a valid Canon of the Mass including Christ's Words of Institution and the Epiklesis.

Christ is truly present in the Eucharist; Body, Blood, Soul and Divinity. Jesus left no room for doubt in His words "This is My Body"…"This Is My Blood" and "do this in *remembrance* of me". Remembrance being understood in the Jewish context of supernaturally revisiting that event, and participating in it, through the spiritual power of God, in a way that we can only simply confess as a mystery of faith.

There can be no communion with an individual who claims to be Christian, yet rejects this mystery of faith, the Real Presence of Christ in the Eucharist. Indeed to partake of the consecrated bread and wine is to sin against the Body and Blood of Christ. "Whoever therefore, eats the bread or drinks the cup of the Lord in an unworthy manner will be guilty of profaning the Body and Blood of the Lord."(1 Cor. 11:27-30)

Apostolic Tradition

In explaining Apostolic Tradition, many Evangelical Protestants immediately begin to think of Christ's condemnation of "traditions of men", and immediately assume that all tradition follows this category; it does not. The term "Apostolic Tradition" does not refer to human customs, practices or ceremonies. Apostolic Tradition is the "Deposit of Faith" "The faith once and for all handed down to the saints" (Jude 3). The word selected by the sacred writer for "handed down" is paradotheise, the root form being paradidomi, from which we derive our English word "tradition". [28] As Tradition is understood in this verse, it refers to the "Deposit of Faith", the Holy Gospel or Good News of Jesus Christ.

Tradition, as defined here, is not man-made, and it is not something apart from Scripture. Apostolic Tradition is God's Word, alive in the living experience and expression of faith of the Body of Christ, the Church. What is an example of Apostolic Tradition? The canon of the New Testament, that is, the recognized list of books that comprise the New Testament is Apostolic Tradition. Indeed, the entire canon of the Bible, of both Old and New Testament, is a matter of Apostolic Tradition, and it is an Apostolic Tradition that must be followed or else you have no Bible. [29] Many books of the Bible do not, in their text, indicate their author, and yet, through Apostolic Tradition, we accept the authorship as given by Apostolic Tradition.

Is this to say that all traditions found in the Church are Apostolic Traditions? To say so, would be to confuse customs (tradition with a small t), with the Deposit of Faith, which is Apostolic teaching (Tradition with a capital T for our discussion).

But let's not forget the Lord's condemnation of the "traditions of men", "Then the Pharisees and scribes came to Jesus and said, 'Why do your disciples transgress the traditions of the elders? For they do not wash their hands when they eat". (Matthew 15:1-2) The washing of the hands was a human restriction imposed by the elders, and not part of any deposit of Divine Revelation. Christ's condemnation too, was of the elders creation of "loopholes" in Mosaic Law to allow the violation of commandments, such as the creation of the "Corban rule" found in Mark 7:9-13. In the "Corban Rule" a son was "lawfully" able to keep money that should have been given to support one's parents in their old age, by claiming that it had been given for use at the Temple, yet maintaining control over it.

Apostolic Tradition then, is not man-made customs or ceremony. In the early years of the Church, the teaching of the Gospel of Christ (which was and is termed the Apostolic Tradition) was done orally, as for about the first three hundred years in the life of the Church, there was not a Bible as we know it today. There was the Jewish Old Testament in the form of the Septuagint and the Apostolic Letters which, at first, circulated to a few, but not all of the early churches. Most people could not read or write, but could listen, and learned the Good News in the same way the Oral Torah had been transmitted to their Jewish forbearers, alongside and with the Written Torah, both as the Word of God.

An interpretation of the written Bible, absent the understanding of the Faith that is conveyed with it, as the Apostolic Tradition, opens the door to an individual, subjective and private approach to interpretation of Scripture that the Bible itself warns us to shun and avoid. Consider the points raised by the following:

> "To separate the Bible from the Church is to make it a 'free-floating' balloon, whereby an endless number of interpreters can blow it in any direction their doctrinal biases please. However, the Spirit-led Church throughout time does not leave room for such a subjective approach. She, through the co-operation of her members, is able to discern God's Word because she is a body, a network of relationships which transcends 'private' interpretations or limited eras. This all-encompassing union is possible because of the unique spiritual bond which exists between the Body of Christ and Jesus the Word.

> God's Word is intended for *God's* people, not for unbelievers. *The Word of God is revealed and experienced as the Word of God only when it is received by a people of faith.* How, then, does the unbeliever hear God's Word? God's Word is spoken to unbelievers *through* believers (either via their testimony in the scriptures, or through those now living). But in either case, God's Word is not heard as God's Word unless the Spirit of the Word reveals it to those who listen. This is why Jerome (342-420) stated that even though the Gnostics had Biblical texts in their possession, they still did not posses the Gospel. For the same reason Tertullian (155-220 AD), a teacher and leader of the African Church, never discussed the Bible with Heretics. They had no right to use the Scriptures....they did not belong to them. Scriptures are the Church's possession." [30]

And even more succinctly;

> "The Bible without the Spirit and Christ's Body is only potentially sufficient. *It is all sufficient only when read within the fellowship of all the saints of all time.* The ministry of Spirit in the Church (Tradition), lets us see the Biblical Message clearly. *Here*, within the Community of God, one can begin to compre-

hend the 'breadth, length, height and depth' of God's love in Christ (Eph. 3:17-19). *Here,* the Scriptures become self-evident to the individual believer. *Here,* they can be understood for what they really are: the revelation of God among His people." [31]

"I hope to come to you soon, but I am writing these instructions to you so that, if I am delayed, you may know how one ought to behave in the household of God, which is the pillar and bulwark of the truth." (1 Tim. 3:14-15) And so it is the Church that is the ultimate arbiter.

And so, Apostolic Tradition is not some foreign concept espoused by the Roman Catholic Church, as many Protestants wrongly believe, it is the understanding of Scriptural understanding, teaching and interpretation, as espoused by all of Christendom, Eastern and Western.

"So then, brethren, stand firm and hold to the Traditions which you were taught by us, either by word of mouth or by letter." (2 Thess. 2:15) Here we see Apostolic Tradition conveyed verbally having the same weight and authority as that which was written down.

Paul instructs Timothy thus: "...you have heard from me before many witnesses entrust to faithful men who will be able to teach others also." (2 Tim 2:2)

"Now we command you, brethren, in the name of our Lord Jesus Christ, that you keep away from any brother who is living in idleness and not in accord with the Tradition that you have received from us." (2 Thess. 3:6)

"Follow the pattern of the sound words which you have heard from me, in the faith and love which are in Christ Jesus; guard the truth that has been entrusted to you by the Holy Spirit who dwells within us." (2 Tim. 1:13-14)

Jesus did not write the New Law on papyrus or skins, He wrote it in the hearts, minds and souls of the Apostles: "Then he opened their minds to understand the Scriptures, and said to them, 'Thus it is written, that the Christ should suffer and on the third day rise from the dead, and that repentance and forgiveness of sins should be preached in his name to all nations, beginning in Jerusalem." (Luke 24:45-47) This Faith, which was taught to us by the Church, lives in each Christian, and is a part of us. To deviate from it is to from the Deposit of Faith inherent in the Church of God. *deviate*

On Apostolic Tradition:

"Of the dogmas and kerygmas preserved in the Church, some we posses from written teaching and others we receive from the tradition of the Apostles, handed on to us in mystery. In respect to piety both are of the same force. No one will contradict any of these, no one, at any rate, who is even moderately versed in matters ecclesiastical. Indeed, were we to try to reject unwritten customs as having no great authority, we would unwittingly injure the Gospel in its vitals; or rather, we would reduce kerygma to a mere term. For instance, to take the first and most general example, who taught us in writing to sign with the sign of the cross those who have trusted in the name of our Lord Jesus Christ? What writing has taught us to turn to the East in prayer? Which of the saints left us in writing the words of the epiclesis at the consecration of the Bread of the Eucharist and the Cup of Benediction?…Where is it written that we are to bless the baptismal water, the oil of anointing, and even the one who is baptized? Is it not from silent and mystical tradition? Indeed, in what written word is even the anointing with oil taught? Where does it say that in baptizing there is to be a triple immersion?" St. Basil the Great, *The Holy Spirit*, 375 A.D. [32]

"It is needful also to make use of Tradition; for not everything can be gotten from Sacred Scripture. The holy Apostles handed down some things in the Scriptures, other things in Tradition." *St. Epiphanius of Salamis, Against All Heresies*, inter 374-377 A.D. [33]

"Therefore, brethren, stand fast and hold to the traditions which you have been taught, whether by word or by our letter.' From this it is clear that they did not hand down everything by letter, but there was much also that was not written. Like that which was written, the unwritten too is worthy of belief. So let us regard the tradition of the Church also as worthy of belief. Is it a tradition? Seek no further." St. John Chrysostom, *Homilies On The Second Epistle To The Thessalonians*, inter 398-404 A.D.

On Abortion:

"You shall not procure abortion, nor destroy a new-born child." *The Didache*, 140 A.D. [34]

"A woman who has deliberately destroyed a fetus must pay the penalty for murder." St. Basil the Great, *Of Basil To Amphilochius, Bishop of Iconium; The First Canonical Letter*, 374 A.D. [30]

On Communion Only To The Baptised:

"Let no one eat or drink of the Eucharist with you except those who have been baptized in the name of the Lord; for it was in reference to this that the Lord said: 'Do not give that which is holy to dogs." *The Didache*, 140 A.D. [35]

On Confession:

"Confess your offenses in church, and do not go up to your prayers with an evil conscience. This is the way of life." *The Didache*, 140 A.D. [36]

"It is necessary to confess our sins to those to whom the dispensation of God's mysteries is entrusted. Those doing penance of old are found to have done it before the saints. It is written in the Gospel that they confessed their sins to John the Baptist; but in Acts they confessed to the Apostles, by whom also all were baptized." St. Basil the Great, *Rules Briefly Treated*, 370 A.D. [37]

"For whatever our transgressions, and whatever we have done through the attacks of the adversary, let us pray that we may be forgiven...For it is good for a man to confess his failings rather than to harden his heart." St. Clement, *Letter To The Corinthians*, 80 A.D. [38]

On Order Within The Church:

"You must all follow the bishop as Jesus Christ follows the Father, and the presbytery as you would the Apostles. Reverence the deacons as you would the command of God. Let no one do anything of concern to the Church without the bishop. Let that be considered a valid Eucharist which is celebrated by the bishop, or by one whom he appoints. Wherever the bishop appears, let the people be there; just as wherever Jesus Christ is, there is the Catholic Church. Nor is it permitted without the bishop either to baptize or to celebrate the agape; but whatever he approve, this too is pleasing to God, so that whatever is done will be secure and valid." St. Ignatius of Antioch, *Letter To The Smyrneans*, 110 A.D.

On The Spiritual Realities Of The Sacraments:

"The Apostle likewise bears witness and says. 'You cannot drink the cup of the Lord and the cup of devils. You cannot be a communicant of the table of the Lord and of the table of devils.' And again he threatens the stubborn and perverse and denounces them, saying: 'Whoever eats the Bread or drinks the Cup of the

Lord unworthily, will be guilty of the Body and Blood of the Lord.' But they spurn and despise all these warnings; and before their sins are expiated, before they have made a confession of their crime, before their conscience has been purged in the ceremony and at the hand of the priest, before the offense against an angry and threatening Lord has been appeased, they do violence to His Body and Blood; and with their hands and mouth they sin against the Lord more than when they denied Him." St. Cyprian of Carthage, *The Lapsed*, 251 A.D.

On Apostolic Succession:

"But since it would be too long to enumerate in such a volume as this the succession of all the Churches, we shall confound all those who, in whatever manner, whether through self-satisfaction or vainglory, or through blindness and wicked opinion, assemble other than where it is proper, by pointing out here the successions of bishops of the greatest and most ancient Church known to all, founded and organized at Rome by the two most glorious Apostles, Peter and Paul, that the church which has the tradition and the faith which comes down to us after having been announced to men by the Apostles. For with this Church, because of its superior origin, all Churches must agree, that is, all the faithful in the whole world; and it is in her that the faithful everywhere have maintained the Apostolic tradition.

The blessed Apostles [Peter and Paul], having founded and built up the Church [of Rome], they handed over the office of the episcopate to Linus. Paul makes mention of this Linus in the Epistle to Timothy. To him succeeded Anencletus; and after him, in the third place from the Apostles, Clement was chosen for the episcopate. He had seen the blessed Apostles and was acquainted with them. It might be said that He still heard the echoes of the preaching of the Apostles, and had their traditions before his eyes. And not only he, for there were many still remaining who had been instructed by the Apostles.

In the time of Clement, no small dissension having arisen among the brethren in Corinth, the Church in Rome sent a very strong letter to the Corinthians, exhorting them to peace and renewing their faith…To this Clement, Evaristus succeeded; and Alexander succeeded Evaristus. Then, sixth after the Apostles, Sixtus was appointed; after him, Telesphorus, who also was gloriously martyred. Then Hyginus; after him, Pius; and after him, Anicetus. Soter succeeded Anicetus, and now, in the twelfth place after the Apostles, the lot of the episcopate has fallen to Eleutherus. In this order, and by the teaching of the Apostles handed down in the

Church, the preaching of the truth has come down to us." St. Irenaeus, *Against Heresies*, inter 180-199 A.D. [39]

On The Essential Belief In The Trinity:

"But what is also to the point, let us note that the very tradition, teaching, and faith of the Catholic Church from the beginning, which the Lord gave, was preached by the Apostles, and was preserved by the Fathers. On this was the Church founded; and if anyone departs from this, he neither is nor any longer ought to be called a Christian: there is a Trinity, holy and perfect, acknowledged as God, in Father, Son and Holy Spirit, having nothing foreign or external mixed with It, not composed of a fashioner and an originated, but entirely creative and fashioning; It is consistent in Itself, indivisible in nature, and Its activity is one." St. Athanasius, *Four Letters To The Serapion of Thmius*, 359-360 A.D. [40]

Faith and Works

True Faith in Christ is a faith that is operative in the life of the believing Christian. An individual who truly believes that Christ is the Messiah acts on that faith, not in order *to* be saved, but because he can, through Christ, be saved. Faith is not a mere intellectual assent to the "concept" of God and salvation, and neither is believing in the Lord. True faith results in a conversion of the individual through this communion with God, and calls the Christian to transfigure his or her life into an expression and extension of Christ's sacrificial life among us. True faith, works. True belief elicits some response from the believer. Even "the demons believe, *and tremble.*"

To those who say that all that is required of an individual is to believe in the Lord, in order to be saved, in order to justify a minimal intrusiveness of God in the daily life of the Christian, the challenge is simply to look at: What does the term 'believe' mean? To answer that question, is to refer to the complete context of Scripture, and not isolate one sentence and take it out of context. In doing so, we see that this one word infers far more than mere intellectual assent.

St. Paul condemned the "*works of the law*", that is, the laws of the Deuteronomic Code, including the sacrifices for atonement for sin, because these requirements did not cleanse sin, they served to bring man face-to-face with his sin, so that he would look forward to the coming of the Messiah, which had come. This is not to be confused with St. James speaking on faith without works being dead. He was speaking of the works of mercy and kindness to one another, as Christians, their lives configured to Christ, should be engaged it. Again, this indicates that a faith that is not operative in the life of the believer is not a true faith.

"What does it profit, my brethren, if a man says he has faith but has not works? Can his faith save him? If a brother or sister is ill-clad and in lack of daily food, and one of you says to them 'Go in peace, be warmed and well filled,' without giving then the things needed for the body, what does it profit? So faith by itself, if it has no works, is dead." (James 2:14-17)

And again:

"You believe that God is one; you do well. Even the demons believe—and shudder. Do you want to be shown, you foolish fellow, that faith apart from works is barren? Was not Abraham our Father justified by works, when he offered his son Isaac upon the altar? You see that faith was active along with his works, and faith was completed by works, and the scripture was fulfilled which says, 'Abraham believed God, and it was reckoned to him as righteousness'; and he was called the friend of God. You see that a man is justified by works and not by faith alone." (James 2:19-24)

"When we hear, 'Your faith has saved you,' we do not understand [the Lord] to say simply that they will be saved who have believed in whatever manner, even if works have not followed. To begin with, it was to the Jews alone that He spoke this phrase, who had lived in accord with the law and blamelessly, and who had lacked only faith in the Lord." St. Clement of Alexandria, *Stromateis or Miscellanies*, post 202 A.D. [41]

"By faith Noah, being warned by God concerning events as yet unseen, took heed and constructed an ark for the saving of his household; by this he condemned the world and became an heir of the righteousness which comes by faith" (Heb. 11:7)

"Do not marvel at this; for the hour is coming when all who are in the tombs will hear his voice and come forth, those who have done good, to the resurrection of life, and those who have done evil, to the resurrection of judgment." (John 5:28-29)

And so, having been given the eternal gift of Divine Sonship, through Christ's sacrifice, we are to take up our cross and follow Him. We must work out our salvation, in fear and trembling (Phil 2:12) and not be proud or arrogant in our adoption into the Divine Family, lest we fall (1 Cor. 9:27). We must walk in faith, and obey Christ not only in word, but also in deed, lest we be cut off from Him (Rom. 11:21-22).

ENDNOTES FOR CHAPTER FOUR

[1] The Most Reverend Joseph Rene Vilatte, *A Sketch of the Belief of Old Catholics*,

[2] Jordan Bajis, *Common Ground, An Introduction to Eastern Christianity For The American Christian*, Second Edition (Light and Life Publishing, 1989)

[3] Ibid, p.171.

[4] Ibid, p.172.

[5] Ibid, p.172-173.

[6] Ibid, p. 173-174.

[7] William A. Jurgens, *The Faith of the Early Fathers Volume 1*, (The Liturgical Press Collegeville, MN, 1970), p. 169.

[8] Ibid. p. 209 vol. 1.

[9] Ibid. p. 233 vol. 1.

[10] Jordan Bajis, *Common Ground, An Introduction to Eastern Christianity For The American Christian*, Second Edition (Light and Life Publishing, 1989), p.218.

[11] Ibid., p.218.

[12] Ibid., p.218.

[13] Ibid, p.218.

[14] Ludwig Ott, *Fundamentals of Catholic Dogma*, (Tan Books and Publishers 1974)

[15] Ibid.

[16] William A. Jurgens, *The Faith of the Early Fathers Volume 1*, (The Liturgical Press Collegeville, MN, 1970) p. 21.

[17] Ibid, p.55, vol. 1.

[18] Ibid, p.99, vol. 1.

19. Joseph Renee Vilatte, *A Sketch of the Belief of Old Catholics,*

20. Arnold Mathew, *Bishop Mathew's Act of Union,* (1911)

21. William A. Jurgens, *The Faith of the Early Fathers Volume 1,* (The Liturgical Press Collegeville, MN, 1970) p. 360 vol. 1.

22. Joseph Renee Vilatte, *A Sketch of the Belief of Old Catholics,*

23. Arnold Mathew, *Bishop Mathew's Act of Union,* (1911)

24. Ibid.

25. Joseph Renee Vilatte, A Sketch of the Belief of Old Catholics,

26. Arnold Mathew, *Bishop Mathew's Act of Union,* (1911)

27. William A. Jurgens, *The Faith of the Early Fathers Volume 1,* (The Liturgical Press Collegeville, MN, 1970) p.231, vol 1.

28. Patrick Madrid, *Why Is That In Tradition?* (Our Sunday Visitor Publishing Division, 2002)

29. Ibid.

30. Jordan Bajis, *Common Ground, An Introduction to Eastern Christianity For The American Christian,* Second Edition (Light and Life Publishing, 1989)

31. Ibid.

32. William A. Jurgens, *The Faith of the Early Fathers,* (The Liturgical Press Collegeville, MN, 1970) p.19, vol. 2.

33. Ibid. p.73, vol. 2.

34. Ibid. p.2, vol. 1.

35. Ibid. p.6, vol. 2.

36. Ibid. p.3, vol. 1.

37. Ibid. p.26, vol. 2.

38. Ibid. p.2, vol. 1.

39. Ibid. p.90, vol. 1.

40. Ibid. p.336, vol. 1.

41. Ibid. p.181

5

A Model Catechism

In this chapter, we look at a model catechism, which is, in this case, the official Catechism of the Old Catholic Church of America. We thank the Old Catholic Church of America and Archbishop James Bostwick, for allowing us to reproduce this detailed catechetical work. This provides an accurate teaching aid and indicator of Old Catholic faith and understanding. This catechism is currently in use by the Old Catholic Church of America, and was adopted and approved for use in instruction within the Old Catholic Church of the United States. This catechism provides a solid foundation for basic instruction as well as offers an opportunity to select specific topics for more detailed study.

Official Catechism[1]

Preliminary Instruction:

Q. What is a catechism?

A. A Catechism is an instruction in the faith, to be taught to all Christians, to enable them to please God, and save their own souls.

Q. What is the meaning of the word catechism?

A. It is a Greek word, signifying instruction, or oral teaching; and has been used ever since the Apostles' times to denote that primary instruction in the Orthodox faith, which is needful for every Christian. **Luke 1:4; Acts 18:25**

Q. What is necessary in order to please God, and save one's own soul?

A. In the first place the knowledge of the true God, and right faith in Him; in the second place, a life according to faith and good works.

Q. Why is faith necessary in the first place?

A. Because, as the word of God testifies, *Without faith it is impossible to please God.* **Heb. 11:6**

Q. Why must a life according to faith, and good works, be inseparable from this faith?

A. Because as the word of God testifies, *faith without works is dead.* **James 2:20**

Q. What is faith?

A. According to the definition of St. Paul, *Faith is the substance of things hoped for, the evidence of things not seen.* **Heb. 11:1** That is, a trust in the unseen, as though it were seen, in that which is hoped and waited for, as if it were present.

Q. What is the difference between knowledge and faith?

A. Knowledge has for its object things visible and comprehensible; faith, things which are invisible and even incomprehensible. Knowledge is founded on experience, on examination of its object; but faith on belief of testimony to truth. Knowledge belongs properly to the intellect, although it may also act on the heart; faith belongs principally to the heart, although it is imparted through the intellect.

Q. Why is faith and knowledge only necessary in religious instruction?

A. Because the chief object of this instruction is God invisible and incomprehensible, and the wisdom of God hidden in a mystery; consequently, many parts of this learning cannot be embraced by knowledge, but may be received by faith.

Faith, says St. Cyril of Jerusalem, is the eye which enlighteneth every man's conscience; it giveth man knowledge. For as the prophet says, If ye will not believe, ye shall not understand. **Isaiah 7:9, Cyr. Cat. V**

On Divine Revelation:

Q. What is the source of the Catholic Faith?

A. Divine Revelation.

Q. What is meant by the words Divine Revelation?

A. That which God Himself has revealed to men, in order that they might rightly and savingly believe in Him, and worthily honor Him.

Q. Has God given such a revelation to all men?

A. He has given it for all, as being necessary for all alike, and capable of bringing salvation to all: but since not all men are capable of receiving a revelation immediately from God, He has employed special persons as heralds of His revelation, to deliver it to all who are desirous of receiving it.

Q. Who were some of the men who received Divine Revelation?

A. Adam, Noah, Abraham, Moses and other Prophets, received and preached the beginnings of divine revelation; but it was the Incarnate Son of God, our Lord Jesus Christ, who brought it to earth in its fullness and perfection, and spread it over all the world by His disciples and Apostles.

The Apostle Paul says in the beginning of his Epistle to the Hebrews: *God, who at sundry times, and in diverse manners, spoke in times past unto the Fathers by the Prophets, hath in these last days spoken unto us by His Son; Whom He hath appointed heir of all things, by Whom also He made the Worlds.* **I Cor. 11:7; John 1:8; Mat. 11:27**

Q. Can man then have some knowledge of God without a special revelation from Him?

A. Man may have some knowledge of God by contemplation of those things He has created; but this knowledge is imperfect and insufficient, and can serve only as a preparation for faith, or as a help towards the knowledge of God from His revelation. *Rom. 1:20; Acts 27:26-2*

On Holy Tradition and Holy Scripture:

Q. How is Divine Revelation spread among men, and preserved in the true Church?

A. By two channels: Holy Tradition and Holy Scripture.

Q. What is meant by the name of Holy Tradition?

A. By the name Holy Tradition is meant the doctrine of faith, the law of God, and the sacraments, has handed down by the true believers and worshippers of God by word and example from one to another, and from generation to generation.

Q. What is the repository of Holy Tradition?

A. All true believers united by holy tradition of the faith, collectively and successively, by the will of God, compose the Church; and She is the sure repository of holy Tradition, or as St. Paul expresses it, *The Church of the living God, the pillar and ground of the truth.* **I Tim. 3:15**

Q. What is that which you call Holy Scripture?

A. Certain books written by the Spirit of God, through men sanctified by God, called Prophets and Apostles. Theses books are commonly termed the Bible.

Q. What does the word Bible mean?

A. It is Greek, and means *The Books*. The name signifies that the sacred books deserve attention before all others.

Q. Which is the more ancient, Holy Tradition, or Holy Scripture?

A. The most ancient and original instrument for spreading Divine Revelation is Holy Tradition. From Adam to Moses there were no sacred books. Our Lord Jesus Christ Himself delivered His Divine doctrine and ordinances to His disciples by word and example, but not the writing. The same method was followed by the Apostles also at first, when they spread abroad the faith and established the Church of Christ. The necessity of tradition is further evident from this, that books can be available only to a small part of mankind, but tradition to all.

Q. Why then was Holy Scripture given?

A. To this end, that Divine Revelation might be preserved more exactly and unchangeably. In Holy Scripture we read the words of the Prophets and Apostles precisely as if we were living with them and listening to them, although the latest of the sacred books were written a thousand and some hundred years before our time.

Q. Must we follow Holy Tradition, even when we possess Holy Scripture?

A. We must follow that tradition which agrees with the Divine Revelation and with Holy Scripture, as is taught is by Holy Scripture itself. The Apostle Paul writes: *Therefore, brethren, stand fast, and hold the traditions which ye have been taught, whether by word or our epistle.* **II Thess. 2:15**

Q. Why is Tradition necessary even now?

A. As a guide to the right understanding of Holy Scripture, and for the right ministration of the Sacraments.

On Holy Scripture in particular:

Q. When were the sacred books written?

A. At different times; some before the birth of Christ, others after.

Q. Have not these two divisions of the sacred books each their own names?

A. They have. Those written before the birth of Christ are called the books of the Old Testament; while those written after are called books of the New Testament.

Q. What are the Old and New testaments?

A. In other words: the old and new agreements of God with men.

Q. Of what does the Old Testament consist?

A. That God promised men a Divine Savior, and prepared them to receive Him.

Q. How did God prepare men to receive the Savior?

A. Through gradual revelations, by prophecies and types.

Q. Of what does the New Testament consist?

A. That God has actually given men a Divine Savior, His only-begotten Son, Jesus Christ.

Q. How many books of the Old Testament are there?

A. Forty-seven.

Q. Is there any division of the books of the Old Testament by which you can give a more distinct account of their contents?

A. They may be divided into the four following classes:
1. Books of the Law, which form the basis of the Old Testament.
2. Historical books, which contain principally the history of religion.
3. Doctrinal, which contain the doctrine of religion.
4. Prophetical, which contain prophecies, or predictions of things future, especially of Jesus Christ.

Q. Which are the books of the Law?

A. The five books written by Moses: Genesis, Exodus, Leviticus, Numbers, and Deuteronomy. Jesus Christ Himself, gives to these books the general name of the Law of Moses. **Luke 24:44**

Q. What in particular is contained in the book of Genesis?

A. The account of the creation of the world and of man, and afterwards the history and ordinances of religion in the first ages of mankind.

Q. What is contained in the other four books of Moses?

A. The history of religion in the time of the Prophet Moses, and the Law given through him from God.

Q. Which are the historical books of the Old Testament?

A. The Books of Joshua, the son of Nun, Judges, Ruth, Kings, Chronicles, the books of Esdras, and the books of Nehemiah, Ester, Tobias, Judith, and Maccabees.

Q. Which are doctrinal?

A. The book of Job, The psalms, the books of Solomon.

Q. What should we remark in particular of the book of psalms?

A. This book, together with the doctrine of religion, contains also allusions to its history, and many prophecies of our Savior Christ. It is a perfect manual of prayer and praise, and on this account is in continual use in the Divine service of the Church.

Q. Which books are prophetical?

A. Those of the Prophets: Isaiah, Jeremiah, Ezekiel, Daniel, the twelve others plus Baruch.

Q. How many books of the New Testament are there?

A. Twenty-seven.

Q. Are there among these any which answer to the books of the Law, or form the basis of the New Testament?

A. Yes. The Gospel, which consist of the four books of the Evangelists Matthew, Mark, Luke, and John.

Q. What does the word Gospel mean?

A. It is the same word as the Greek word Evangel, and means good and joyful news.

Q. Of what have we good news in the books called the Gospel?

A. Of the Divinity of our Lord Jesus Christ, of His advent and life on earth, of His miracles and saving doctrine, and finally, of His death upon the cross, His glorious resurrection, and Ascension into heaven.

Q. Why are these books called the Gospel?

A. They are called Gospel because man can have no better nor more joyful news than these, of a Divine Savior and everlasting salvation. For the same cause, whenever the Gospel is read in the Church, it is prefaced and accompanied by joyful exclamation: *Glory be to Thee, O Lord. Glory be to Thee.*

Q. Are any of the books of the New Testament historical?

A. Yes. One; the book of the Acts of the Holy Apostles.

Q. Of what does it give an account?

A. Of the descent of the Holy Spirit on the Apostles, and the extension through them of Christ's Church.

Q. What is an Apostle?

A. The word means a messenger. It is the name given to those disciples of our Lord Jesus Christ, whom He sent to preach the Gospel.

Q. Which books of the New Testament are doctrinal?

A. The seven General Epistles; namely, one of the Apostle James, two of Peter, three of John, and one of Jude; and fourteen Epistles of the Apostle Paul: namely, one to the Romans, two to the Corinthians, one to the Galatians, one to the Ephesians, one to the Philippians, one to the Colossians, two to the Thessalonians, two to Timothy, one to Titus, one to Philemon, and one to the Hebrews.

Q. Are there also among the books of the New Testament any prophetical?

A. Such is the book of the Apocalypse, which means Revelation.

Q. What are the contents of this book?

A. A mystical representation of the future destinies of the Christian Church, and of the whole world.

Q. What rules must we observe in reading Holy Scripture?

A. First, we must read it devoutly, as the Word of God, and with prayer to understand it right; secondly, we must read it with a pure desire of instruction in faith, and incitement to good works; thirdly, we must take and understand it in such sense as agrees with interpretation of the Church and the holy fathers.

OFFICIAL CATECHISM
THE FIRST PART: ON FAITH

On the Creed Generally, and on its Origin:

Q. What is the Nicene Creed?

A. The Nicene Creed is a summary of that doctrine which all Christians are bound to believe.

Q. What are the 12 divisions of the Creed?

A. They are as follows:

1. I believe in one God the Father, Almighty, Maker of heaven and earth, and of all things visible and invisible;

2. And in one Lord Jesus Christ, the Son of God, the only-begotten, begotten of the Father before all worlds, Light of Light, very God of very God, begotten, not made of one substance with the Father, by whom all things were made;

3. Who for us men, and for our salvation, came down from heaven, and was incarnate of the Holy Spirit, and of the Virgin Mary, and was made man;

4. And was crucified also for us, under Pontius Pilate, and suffered, and was buried.

5. And rose again the third day according to the Scripture;

6. And ascended into heaven, and sitteth on the right hand of the Father;

7. And He shall come again with glory to judge the living and the dead, whose kingdom shall have no end.

8. And I believe in the Holy Spirit, the Lord, the Giver of Life, who proceedeth from the Father, who with the Father and the Son together is worshipped and glorified, who spoke by the Prophets.

9. I believe one Holy, Catholic, and Apostolic Church.

10. I acknowledge one baptism for the remission of sins.

11. I look for the resurrection of the dead;

12. And the life of the world to come. Amen.

Q. From whom have we this summary of the Faith?

A. From the Fathers of the First and Second Ecumenical Councils.

Q. What is an Ecumenical Council?

A. An assembly of the Bishops and theologians of the Catholic Church, as far as possible, from the whole world, for the confirmation of true doctrine and practice among Christians.

Q. How many Ecumenical Councils have there been?

A. Seven: 1) Nicea; 2) Constantinople; 3) Ephesus; 4) Chalcedon; 5) The second of Constantinople; 6) The third of Constantinople; 7) The second of Nicea.

Q. What evidence is there in Scripture for holding Ecumenical Councils?

A. From the example of the Apostles, who held a Council in Jerusalem. *Acts 15.* This is grounded also upon the words of Jesus Christ Himself, which give to the decisions of the Church such weight, that whoever disobeys them is left deprived of grace. The means by which the Catholic Church utters her decisions is an Ecumenical Council. **Mat. 28:17**

Q. What were the particular occasions for assembling the First and Second Ecumenical Councils, at which the Creed was defined?

A. The first was held for the confirmation of the true doctrine respecting the Son of God, against the error of Arius; the second for the confirmation of the true doctrine respecting the Holy Spirit, against Macedonius.

On the Articles of the Creed:

Q. What method shall we follow in order the better to understand the Nicene Creed?

A We must notice its division into twelve articles or parts, and consider each article separately.

Q. What is spoken of in each article of the Creed?

A. The first article of the Creed speaks of God as the prime origin, more particularly of the first Person of the Holy Trinity, God the Father, and of God as Creator of the World;

The second article, of the Second Person of the Holy Trinity, Jesus Christ, the Son of God;

The third article, of the incarnation of the Son of God;

The fourth article, of the suffering and death of Jesus Christ;

The fifth article, of the resurrection of Jesus Christ;

The sixth article, of the Ascension of Jesus Christ into heaven;

The seventh article, of the second coming of Jesus Christ upon earth;

The eighth article, of the third person of the Holy Trinity, the Holy Spirit:

The ninth article, of the Church;

The tenth article, of Baptism, under which are implied the other Sacraments also;

The eleventh article, of the future resurrection of the dead;

The twelfth article, of the life everlasting.

On the First Article:

Q. What does it mean to believe in God?

A. To believe in God is to have a lively belief in His being, His attributes, and worlds; and to receive with all our heart His revealed word for the salvation of men.

Without faith it is impossible to please God; for he that cometh to God must believe that He is, and that He is a rewarder of the that diligently seek Him. **Heb.11:6 Eph. 3:16,17**

Q. What must be the immediate and constant effect of a firm faith in God?

A. The confession of this same faith.

Q. What is the confession of this faith?

A. It is openly to show that we hold the Catholic faith, and this with such sincerity and firmness, that neither force, nor threats, nor tortures, nor death itself, may be able to make us deny our faith in the true God and in our Lord Jesus Christ.

Q. For what reason is the confession of the faith necessary?

A. The Apostle Paul witnesses that it is necessary for salvation. *For with the heart man believeth unto righteousness, and with the mouth confession is made unto salvation.* **Rom. 10:10**

Q. What does Holy Scripture teach us of the unity of God?

A. The very words of the Creed on this point are taken from the following passage of the Apostle Paul: *There is none other God but one. For though there be they that are called gods, whether in heaven or on earth, as there be gods many, and lords many, but to us there is but one God, the Father, of whom are all things, and we in Him: and one Lord Jesus Christ, by whom are all things, and we by Him.* **I Cor. 7:4-6**

Q. Can we know the very essence of God, or God as He is?

A. No. It is above all knowledge, not men only, but of Angels. The apostle Paul says that God *dwelleth in the light, which no man can approach unto, Whom no man hath seen, nor can see.* **I Tim.6:16**

Q. What are some of the attributes of God?

A. God is a Spirit, eternal, all-good, all knowing, all-just, almighty, all present, unchangeable, all-sufficing to Himself, all-blessed.

Q. If God is a Spirit, how does Holy Scripture ascribe to Him bodily parts, as heart, eyes, ears, hands.

A. Holy Scripture in this suits itself to the common language of men; but we are to understand such expression in a higher and spiritual sense. For instance, the heart of God means His goodness or his love; eyes and ears mean His omniscience: hands, His almighty power.

Q. If God is everywhere, why do men say that God is in heaven, or in the church?

A. God is everywhere: but in heaven He has a special presence manifested in everlasting glory to the blessed spirits; also in churches He has, through grace and Sacraments, a special presence devoutly recognized and felt by believers, and manifested sometimes by extraordinary signs.

Jesus Christ says: *Where two or three are gathered together in my name, there am I in the midst of them.* **Mat. 28:20**

Q. How are we to understand these words of the Creed, *I belive in one God the Father?*

A. This is to be understood with reference to the mystery of the Holy Trinity; because God is one in substance, but three in persons, the Father, the Son, and the Holy Spirit. *I John 5:7*

Q. Is the Holy Trinity mentioned in the Old Testament also?

A. Yes; only not as clearly. For instance. *By the Word of the Lord were the heavens made, and all the hosts of them by the breath of his mouth.* **Psalm 33:6** *Holy, Holy, Holy is the Lord of Hosts: The whole earth is full of His glory.* **Isaiah 6:3**

Q. How is God one in three Persons?

A. We cannot understand this inner mystery of the Godhead; but we believe it on the infallible testimony of the word of God. *The things of God knoweth no man, but the Spirit of God.* **I Cor. 2:11**

Q. What difference is there between the Persons of the Holy Trinity?

A. God the Father is neither begotten, nor proceeds from any other Person: the Son of God is from all eternity begotten of the Father: the Holy Spirit from all eternity proceeds from the Father.

Q. Are the three Persons of the Most Holy Trinity all of equal majesty?

A. Yes. All are equally God. The Father is true God; the Son equally true God; and the Holy Spirit true God; but in three Persons there is only one God.

Q. Why is God called Almighty?

A. Because He upholds all things by His power and His will.

Q. What is expressed by the words of the Creed, *Maker of heaven and earth, and of all things visible and invisible?*

A. That all was made by God, and that nothing can be without God. The book of Genesis begins thus: *In the beginning God created the heaven and the earth.* The Apostle Paul speaking of Jesus Christ, the Son of God says: *By Him were all things created, that are in heaven, and that are in earth, visible and invisible, whether they be thrones, or dominions, or principalities, or powers; all things were created by Him, and for Him.* **Coloss. 1:16**

Q. What is meant in the Creed by the word invisible?

A. The invisible or spiritual world, to which belong the Angels.

Q. What are the Angels?

A. Angels are Spirits, having intelligence, will, and power, but no material bodies.

Q. What does the name Angel mean?

A. It means a <u>Messenger</u>.

Q. Why are they so called?

A. Because God sends them to announce His will. Thus for instance, Gabriel was sent to announce to the Most Holy Virgin Mary the conception of the Savior.

Q. Which was created first, the visible world or the invisible?

A. The invisible was created before the visible, and the Angels before men. *Who laid the corner-stone thereof? When the stars were created, all My Angels praised Me with a loud voice.* **Job 38:6,7**

Q. Where in Scripture are Guardian Angels mentioned?

A. In Psalm 91: 11: *He shall give His Angels charge over thee, to guard thee in all thy ways.*

Q. Has each one of us a Guardian Angel?

A. Yes. Of this we may be assured from the following words of Jesus Christ: *Take heed that ye despise not one of these little ones: for I say unto you, that in heaven their Angels do always behold the face of my Father, which is in heaven.* **Mat. 18:10**

Q. Are all Angels good and protective?

A. No. There are also evil angels, otherwise called devils.

Q. How did they become evil?

A. They were created good, but they swerved from their duty of perfect obedience to God, and so fell away from Him into self-will, pride, and malice. According to the words of the Apostle Jude, *they are the Angels which kept not their first estate, but left their own habitation.* **Jude 6**

Q. What does the name devil mean?

A. It means slanderer or deceiver.

Q. Why are the evil angels called devils, that is, slanderers or deceivers.

A. Because they are ever laying snares for men, seeking to deceive them, and mislead them with false notions and evil wishes.

Q. What has Holy Scripture revealed to us of the creation of the world?

A. In the beginning God created from nothing the heaven and the earth, and all that they contain. Afterwards God successively produced: on the first day of the world, light; on the second, the firmament or visible heaven; on the third, the gathering together of the waters on the earth, the dry land, and what grows thereupon; on the fourth, the sun, moon, and stars; on the fifth, fishes and birds; on the sixth, four-footed creatures living on the earth, and lastly man. With man the creation finished: and on the seventh day was called the Sabbath, which in the Hebrew tongue means rest. **Gen. 2**

Q. Were the visible creatures created such as we see them now?

A. No. At creation everything was very good; that is, pure, beautiful, and harmless.

Q. Are we not informed of something particular in the creation of man?

A. God in the Holy Trinity said: *Let Us make man in Our image, and after Our likeness,* **Gen. 1:26** *And God made the body of the first man, Adam, from the earth: breathed into his nostrils the breath of life: brought him into Paradise; gave him for food, beside the other fruits of Paradise, the fruit of the tree of life: and lastly, having taken a rib from Adam while he slept, made from it the first woman, Eve.* **Gen 2:22**

Q. What is meant by the image of God?

A. The Image of God consists, as explained by the Apostle Paul, *In righteousness and holiness of truth.* **Eph. 4:24**

Q. What is the breath of life?

A. The soul, a substance spiritual and immortal.

Q. What is Paradise?

A. The word Paradise means garden. It is the name given to the fair and blissful dwelling place of the first man, described in the book of Genesis as like a garden.

Q. Was the Paradise in which man first lived material or spiritual?

A. For the body it was material. A visible and blissful dwelling place; but for the soul it was spiritual, a state of communion by grace with God, and spiritual contemplation of the creatures.

Q. What was the tree of life?

A. A tree, by feeding on whose fruit man would have been, even in the body, free from disease and death.

Q. Why was Eve made from a rib of Adam?

A. To the intent that all mankind might be by origin naturally disposed to love and care for one another.

Q. For what purpose did God create man?

A. That he should know God, love, and glorify Him, and so be happy forever.

Q. What is divine providence?

A. Divine providence is the constant energy of the almighty power, wisdom, and goodness of God, by which He preserves the being and faculties of His creatures, directs them to good ends, and assists all that is good; but the evil that springs by departure from good either cuts off, or corrects it, and turns it to good results in cooperation with the goodwill of men.

Behold the fowls of the air, for they sow not, neither do they reap, nor gather into barns, yet your heavenly Father feedeth them. Are ye not much better than they? **Mat. 6:26** From these words is shown at once God's general providence over creatures, and His special providence over man.

On the Second Article:

Q. How are we to understand the name *Jesus Christ, the Son of God*?

A. Son of God is the name of the second person of the Holy Trinity in respect to His Godhead: This same Son of God was called Jesus, when He was conceived and born on earth as man: Christ is the name given Him by the Prophets, while they were as yet expecting His advent upon earth.

Q. What does the name Jesus mean?

A. Savior.

Q. By whom was the name Jesus first given?

A. By the Angel Gabriel.

Q. Why was this name given to the Son of God at His conception and birth on earth?

A. Because He was conceived and born to save men.

Q. What does the name Christ mean?

A. Anointed One.

Q. Is it only Jesus the Son of God who is called Anointed?

A. No. <u>Anointed</u> was in Old Testament times a title of Kings, High Priests, and Prophets.

Q. Why then is Jesus the Son of God called Anointed?

A. Because to His manhood were imparted without measure all the gifts of the Holy Spirit, and so He possesses in the highest degree the knowledge of a Prophet, the holiness of a High Priest, and power of a King.

Q. In what sense is Jesus Christ called Lord?

A. In this sense, that He is truly God; for the name Lord is one of the names of God. *In the Beginning was the Word, and the Word was with God, and the Word was God.* **John 1:1**

Q. Why is Jesus called the Only-begotten Son of God?

A. Because He alone is the Son of God begotten of the substance of God the Father, and so is of one substance with the Father. **John 1:12**

The Word was made flesh, and dwelt among us, and we beheld His glory, the glory as of the Only-begotten of the Father, full of grace and truth. John 1: 14. *No man hath seen God at any time: the Only-begotten Son, which is in the bosom of the Father, He hath declared Him.* **ib. 18**

Q. Why in the Creed is it said further of the Son of God that He is begotten of the Father?

A. By this is expressed that personal property, by which He is distinguished from the other Persons of the Holy Trinity.

Q. Why is it said that He is begotten before all worlds?

A. That none should think there was ever a time when He was not. In other words, by this is expressed that Jesus Christ is the Son of God from all eternity, even as God the Father is from all eternity.

Q. What do the words *Light of Light* mean in the Creed?

A. Under the figure of the visible light they in some manner explain the incomprehensible generation of the Son of God from the Father. When we look at the sun, we see light: from this light is generated the light visible everywhere beneath: but both the one and the other is one light, indivisible and of one nature. In like manner, God the Father is the everlasting Light: **I John 1:5**. Of Him is begotten the Son of God, Who also is the everlasting Light: the God the Father and God the Son are one and the same everlasting Light, indivisible, and of one Divine nature.

Q. What force is there in the words of the Creed, God of God?

A. That the Son of God is called God in the same proper sense as God the Father. *We know that the Son of God is come, and hath given us (light and) understanding, that we may know the true God, and be in Him that is true, in His Son Jesus Christ: This is the true God and eternal life.* **I John 5:20**

Q. Why is it further added of the Son of God in the Creed that he is begotten, not made?

A. This was added against the Arian heresy which incorrectly taught that the Son of God was made.

Q. What do the words *Of one substance with the Father* mean?

A. They mean that the Son of God is of one and the same Divine being with God the Father. *I and the Father are one.* **John 9:30**

Q. What is shown in the next words in the Creed, *By whom all things were made*?

A. That God the Father created all things by His Son, as by His eternal Wisdom and His eternal Word. *All things were made by Him, and without Him was not any thing made which was made.* **John 1:3**

On the Third Article:

Q. What do we mean when we say that He came down from heaven, seeing that as God He is everywhere?

A. It is true that He is everywhere: and so He is always in heaven, and always on earth; but on earth He was without a human body; afterwards He appeared in the flesh; in this sense it is said that *He came down from heaven. No man hath ascended up to heaven, but He that came down from heaven, even the Son of man, which is in heaven.* **John 3:13**

Q. For what reason did the Son of God come down from heaven?

A. *For us men, and for our salvation,* as it is said in the Creed.

Q. In what sense, is it said that the Son of God came down from heaven for us men?

A. In this sense, that He came upon earth not for one nation nor for some men only, but for us men universally.

Q. From what did Christ wish to save us?

A. From sin, the curse, and death.

Q. What is sin?

A. *Sin is the transgression of the law.* **I John 3:8**

Q. How did sin pass from the devil to men?

A. The devil deceived Eve and Adam, and tempted them to break God's commandment.

Q. What commandment?

A. God commanded Adam in Paradise not to eat of the fruit of the *Tree of the knowledge of good and evil,* and also told him that if he ate of it, he would die.

Q. Why did it bring death to man to eat of the fruit of the *Tree of the knowledge of good and evil*?

A. Because it involved disobedience to God's will, and so separated man from God and His grace, and alienated him from the life of God.

Q. What is meant by the *Tree of the knowledge of good and evil*?

A. Man through this tree came to know by the act itself what good there is in obeying the will of God, and what evil there is in disobeying it.

Q. How could Adam and Eve listen to the devil against the will of God?

A. God of His goodness, at the creation of man, gave him a will naturally disposed to love God, but still free; and man used this freedom for evil.

Q. How did the devil deceive Adam and Eve?

A. Eve saw in Paradise a serpent, which assured her that if men ate of the fruit of the tree of the knowledge of good and evil, they would know good and evil, and would become gods. Eve was deceived by this promise and ate of it. Adam ate after her example.

Q. What came of Adam's sin?

A. The curse and death.

Q. What is the curse?

A. The condemnation of sin by God's just judgment, and the evil which from sin came upon the earth for the punishment of men. God said to Adam, *Cursed is the ground for thy sake.* **Gen. 3:17**

Q. What is the death which came from the sin of Adam?

A. It is two fold: Bodily, when the body loses the soul which gives it life; and spiritual, when the soul loses the grace of God, which gives it the higher and spiritual life.

Q. Can the soul then die, as well as the body?

A. It can die, but not in the same way as the body. The body, when it dies loses sense, and is dissolved; the soul, when it dies by sin, loses spiritual light, joy, and happiness, but is not dissolved nor annihilated, but remains in a state of suffering, anguish, and darkness.

Q. Why must all men share the effects of Adam's sin?

A. Because all have descended from Adam, thereby sharing the consequences of sin, and all sin themselves. *By one man sin entered into the world, and death by sin, and so death passed upon all men, for that all have sinned.* **Rom. 5:12**

Q. Did men have any hope left for salvation?

A. When our first parents had confessed before God their sin, God, of His mercy, gave them hope for salvation.

Q. What was this hope?

A. God promised, that the *seed of the woman should bruise the serpent's head.* **Gen. 3:15**

Q. What did that mean?

A. It meant that Jesus Christ should overcome the devil who had deceived men, and deliver them from sin, the curse, and death.

Q. Why is Jesus Christ called *the seed of the woman?*

A. Because he was born on earth without a father from the Most Holy Virgin Mary.

Q. What benefit was there in this promise?

A. The benefit was that from the time of the promise men could believe savingly in the Savior that was to come, even as we now believe in the Savior who has come.

Q. Did people in fact from the Old Testament believe in the Savior that was to come?

A. Some did, but the greater part forgot God's promise of a Savior.

Q. Did not God repeat this promise?

A. More than once. For instance, He made to Abraham the promise of a Savior in the following words: *In thy seed all the nations of the earth be blessed.* **Gen 22:18** The same promise He repeated afterwards to David in the following words: *I will set up thy seed after thee, and I will establish His throne for ever.* **II Kings 7:12,13**

Q. What do we understand by the word <u>Incarnation</u>?

A. That the Son of God took upon Himself human flesh without sin, and was made man, without ceasing to be God. *The Word was made flesh.* **John 1:14**

Q. Why in the Creed, after it has been said of the Son of God that He was incarnate, is it further added that He was made man?

A. To the end that none should imagine that the Son of God took only flesh or a body, but should acknowledge in Him a perfect man consisting of body and soul. *There is one Mediator between God and men, the man Christ Jesus.* **I Tim. 2:5**

Q. And so is there only one nature in Jesus Christ?

A. No; there are in Him without separation and without confusion two natures, the Divine and the human, and with these two natures, two wills.

Q. Are there not therefore also two persons?

A. No; One person, God and man together; in one word, a God-man. The Evangelist Luke relates that when the Virgin Mary had asked the Angel, who announced to her the conception of Jesus, *How shall this be, seeing I know not a man?* The Angel replied to her, *The Holy Spirit shall come upon thee, and the power of the highest shall overshadow thee; therefore also that Holy thing which shall be born of thee shall be called the Son of God.* **Luke 1:34,35**

Q. Who was the Virgin Mary?

A. A holy virgin of the ancestry of Abraham and David, from whose line the Savior, by God's promise, was to come; betrothed to Joseph, a man of the same line, in order that he might be her guardian; for she was dedicated to God with a vow of perpetual virginity.

Q. Did Mary remain, in fact, a virgin?

A. She remained a virgin before the birth, during the birth, and after the birth of the Savior; and therefore, is called ever-virgin.

Q. What other great title is there with which the Church honors the Holy Virgin Mary?

A. That of Mother of God.

Q. Can you show the origin of this title in Holy Scripture?

A. It is taken from the following words of the Prophet Isaiah: *Behold, a virgin shall conceive, and bear a Son, and they shall call his name Emmanuel, which being interpreted, is God with us.* **Isaiah 7:14, Mat. 1:23**

So also the righteous Elizabeth calls the Most Holy Virgin *The Mother of the Lord*; which title is all one with that of Mother of God, *Whence is this to me, that the Mother of my Lord should come to me?* **Luke 1:43**

Q. In what sense is the Most Holy Virgin called Mother of God?

A. Although Jesus Christ was born of her not in His divinity, but of his humanity, still she is rightly called Mother of God, because He that was born of her as a man is nevertheless God.

Q. What thoughts should we have of the exalted dignity of the Most Holy Virgin Mary?

A. As Mother of the Lord she is higher than all created beings in grace and nearness to God.

Q. Give examples of how God prepared His people to know the Saviour when He would be born.

A. The prophet Isaiah foretold that the Saviour should be born of a virgin. **Is. 7:14** The Prophet Micah foretold that the Saviour should be born in Bethlehem; and this prophecy the Jews understood even before they heard of its fulfillment. **Mat. 2:4-6** The Prophet Malachi, after the building of the second temple at Jerusalem, foretold that the coming of the Saviour was drawing near, that He should come to this temple, and that before Him should be sent a forerunner who would be like the Prophet Elias, clearly pointing by this to John the Baptist. **Mal 3:1; 4:5** The Prophet Zachariah foretold the triumphal entry of the Saviour into Jerusalem. **Zach. 9:9** The Prophet Isaiah with wonderful clearness foretold the sufferings of the Saviour. **Is 53** David, in the 23rd Psalm, described the sufferings of the Saviour on the cross itself. And Daniel, 490 years before, foretold the appearance of the Saviour, His death on the cross, and the subsequent destruction of the temple of Jerusalem, and abolition of the Old Testament sacrifices. **Dan. 9**

Q. Did men, in fact, recognize Jesus Christ as the Saviour at the time that He was born and lived upon earth?

A. Many did recognize Him by various ways. The wise men of the East recognized Him by a star, which before His birth appeared in the East. The shepherds of Bethlehem knew of Him from Angels, who distinctly told them that the saviour was born in the city of David. Simeon and Anna, by special revelation of the Holy Spirit, knew Him when He was brought, forty days after His birth, into the temple. John the baptist, at the river Jordan, at His baptism, knew Him by revelation, by the descent of the Holy Spirit upon Him in the form of a dove, and by a voice from heaven from God the Father; *This is My beloved Son, in Whom I am well pleased; hear Him.* **Mark 9:7** Besides this, very many recognized Him by His preaching, and especially by the miracles which He worked.

Q. What are some of the miracles of Jesus Christ?

A. People suffering under incurable diseases, and possessed by devils, were healed by Him in the twinkling of an eye, by a single word, or by the touch of His hand, and even through their touching His garment. Once with five, and another time with seven loaves He fed in the wilderness several thousand men. He walked on the waters, and by a word calmed the storm. He raised the dead; The son of the widow of Nain, the daughter of Jairus, and Lazarus on the fourth day after his death.

Q. How does Christ save us?

A. By His teaching, His life, His death, and resurrection.

Q. What was Christ's main teaching?

A. The Gospel of the Kingdom of God, or in other words, the doctrine of salvation and eternal happiness. **Mark 1:14,15**

Q. How are we saved by Christ's teachings?

A. When we receive it with all our heart, and walk according to it. For, as the false words of the devil, received by our first parents, became in them the seed of sin and death, so, on the contrary, the true word of Christ, sincerely received by Christians, becomes in them the seed of a holy and immortal life. They are, in the words of the Apostle Peter, *born again, not of corruptible seed, but of incorruptible, by the word of God which liveth and abideth for ever.* **I Pet. 1:23**

Q. How do we receive salvation by Christ's life?

A. When we imitate it. For He says, *If anyone serve Me, let Him follow Me; and where I am, there shall also My servant be.* **John 12:26**

On the Fourth Article:

Q. How did it come to pass that Jesus Christ was crucified when His teaching and works should have moved all to love Him?

A. The elders of the Jews and the scribes, who represent all unrepentant sinners, hated Him because He rebuked their false doctrine and evil lives, and envied Him because the people who heard Him teach and saw His miracles respected Him more than them; and hence they falsely accused Him and condemned Him to death.

Q. Why is it said that Jesus Christ was crucified under Pontius Pilate?

A. To mark the time of when He was crucified.

Q. Who was Pontius Pilate?

A. The Roman governor of Judea, which had become subject to the Romans.

Q. Why is this circumstance worthy of remark?

A. Because in it we see the fulfillment of Jacob's prophecy: *The scepter Shall not depart from Judah, nor a lawgiver from between his feet, until Shiloh come: and He is the desire of the nations.* **Gen. 44:10**

Q. Why is it not only said in the Creed that Jesus Christ was crucified, but also added that He suffered?

A. To show that His crucifixion was not only a resemblance of suffering and death, as some have said, but a real suffering and death.

Q. Why is it also mentioned that He was buried?

A. This likewise is to assure us that He really died, and rose again; for His enemies even set a watch at His sepulchre, and sealed it.

Q. How could Jesus Christ suffer and die when He was God?

A. He suffered and died not in His Godhead, but in His manhood; and He did this not because He could not avoid it, but because it pleased Him to suffer for our salvation.

He Himself had said: *I lay down My life, that I may take it again. No man taketh it from Me, but I lay it down for Myself. I have power to lay it down, and I have power to take it again.* **John 10:17,18**

Q. In what sense is it said, that Jesus Christ was crucified for us?

A. That He, by His death on the cross, delivered us from sin, the curse, and death. **Ephes. 1:7; Gal. 3:13; Heb. 2:14,15**

Q. According to Scripture how does the death of Jesus Christ upon the cross deliver us from sin, the curse, and death?

A. *God hath willed to make known to His saints, what is the riches of the glory of this mystery of the Gentiles, which is Christ in you, the hope of glory.* **Col. 1:26,27**

For if by one man's offense death reigned by one, much more they which receive abundance of grace and of the gift of righteousness shall reign in life by one, Jesus Christ. **Rom. 5:17**

There is therefore now no condemnation to them which are in Christ Jesus, who walk not after the flesh but after the spirit. For the law of the spirit of life in Christ Jesus hath made me free from the law of sin and death. For what the law could not do, in that it was weak through the flesh, God sending His own Son in likeness of sinful flesh, and for sin, condemned sin in the flesh; that the righteousness of the law might be fulfilled in us, who walk not after the flesh, but after the spirit. **Rom. 7:1-4**

Q. Did Jesus Christ suffer and die for all men?

A. For His part, He offered Himself as a sacrifice strictly for all, and obtained for all grace and salvation; but this benefits only those of us, who, for our parts, of our own free will, have *fellowship in His sufferings, being made conformable unto His death.* **Philipp. 3:10**

Q. How can we have fellowship in the sufferings and death of Jesus Christ?

A. We have fellowship in the sufferings and death of Jesus Christ through a lively and sincere faith, through the Sacraments, in which is contained and sealed the virtue of His saving sufferings and death, and lastly, through the crucifixion of our flesh with its lusts. **Gal. 2:19,20; Rom. 6:3; I Cor.11:26; Gal. 5:24**

Q. How can we crucify the flesh with its lusts?

A. By doing what is contrary to them. For instance, when anger prompts us to insult an enemy and to do him harm, but we resist the desire, and, remembering how Jesus Christ on the cross prayed for His enemies, pray likewise for ours, we crucify the sin of anger.

On the Fifth Article:

Q. What is the proof given by Jesus Christ, that His sufferings and death have brought salvation to us men?

A. That He rose again, and so laid the foundation for our blessed resurrection. *Now is Christ risen from the dead, and become the first-fruits of them that slept.* **I Cor. 15:20**

Q. What is <u>hades</u> or <u>hell</u> as used in the Creed?

A. Hades is a Greek word, and means a place void of light. In the Creed by this name is understood a spiritual prison, that is, the state of those spirits which are separated by sin from the sight of God's countenance, and from the light and blessedness which it confers. **Jude 1:6**

Q. For what reason did Jesus Christ descend into hell?

A. So that He might there also preach His victory over death, and deliver the souls which with faith awaited His coming. *For Christ also hath once suffered for sins, the just for the unjust, that He may bring us to God, being put to death in the flesh, but quickened in the Spirit: in which also He went and preached unto the Spirits in Prison.* **I Pet. 3:18,19**

Q. What do we mean by the words of the Creed, *and rose again the third day according to the Scripture*?

A. These words were put into the Creed from the following passage in the Epistle to the Corinthians: *For I delivered unto you first of all that which I also received, how that Christ died for our sins, according to the Scripture; and that He was buried, and that He rose again the third day, according to the Scripture.* **I Cor. 15:3,4**

Q. What force is there in these words, *according to the Scripture*?

A. By this is shown that Jesus Christ died and rose again, precisely as had been written of Him prophetically in the books of the Old Testament.

Q. Where for instance, is there anything written of this event?

A. In the 53rd chapter of the book of the Prophet Isaiah, for instance, the suffering and death of Jesus Christ is shown forth with many particular traits; as, *He was wounded for our transgressions, He was bruised for our iniquities; the chastisement of our peace was upon Him; and with His stripes we are healed.* **Isa. 5**

Of the Resurrection of Christ the Apostle Peter quotes the words of the 16th Psalm: *For why? Thou shalt not leave My soul in hell, neither shalt Thou suffer Thy holy one to see corruption.* **Acts 2:27**

Q. Is this also the Scripture of the Old Testament, that Jesus Christ should rise again on the third day?

A. A prophetic type of this was set forth in the Prophet Jonah: *And Jonah was in the belly of the fish three days and three nights.* **John 1:17**

Q. How was it known that Jesus Christ had risen?

A. The soldiers who watched His sepulchre knew this, because an angel of the Lord rolled away the stone which closed His sepulchre, and at the same time there was a great earthquake. Angels likewise announced the Resurrection of Christ to Mary Magdalene and some others. Jesus Christ Himself on the very day of His Resurrection appeared to many; also to the women bringing spices, to Peter, to the two disciples going to Emmaus, and lastly, to all the Apostles in the house, the doors being shut. Afterwards He often showed Himself to them during the span of forty days; and one day, He was seen by more than five hundred believers at one time. **I Cor. 15:6**

Q. What did Jesus Christ after His resurrection continue to teach the Apostles?

A. He continued to teach them the mysteries of the Kingdom of God. **Acts 1:3**

On the Sixth Article:

Q. Is the statement of our Lord's Ascension in the sixth article of the Creed taken from Scripture?

A. It is taken from the following passage of Holy Scripture: *He that descended is the same also that ascended up far above all heavens, that He might fill all things.* **Eph. 4:10**

We have such a High Priest, who is set on the right hand of the throne of the majesty in the heavens. **Heb. 8:1**

Q. Was it in His Godhead or His manhood that Jesus Christ ascended into heaven?

A. In His manhood. In His Godhead He ever was and is in heaven.

Q. How does Jesus Christ *sit at the right hand of God the Father,* **seeing that God is everywhere?**

A. This must be understood spiritually; that is, Jesus Christ has one and the same majesty and glory with God the Father, humanity having been exalted in His Divinity.

On the Seventh Article:

Q. How does Holy scripture speak of Christ's coming again?

A. *This Jesus which is taken up from you into heaven, shall so come in like manner as ye have seen Him go in to heaven.* **Acts 1:2** This was said to the Apostles by angels at the time of our Lord's Ascension.

Q. How does it speak of the future judgment?

A. *The hour is coming, in which all that are in the graves shall hear the voice of the Son of God, and shall come forth; they that have done good, unto the resurrection of life, and they that have done evil, unto the resurrection of damnation.* **John 5:28,29** These are the words of Christ Himself.

Q. How does it speak of His kingdom which is to have no end?

A. *He shall be great, and shall be called the Son of the Highest; and the Lord God shall give unto Him the throne of His father David, and He shall reign over the house of Jacob for ever, and of His kingdom there shall be no end.* **Luke 1:32,33** These are the words of the angel to the Mother of God.

Q. Will the second coming of Christ be like His first?

A. No, it will be different. He came to suffer for us in great humility, but He shall come to judge us *in His glory, and all the holy angels with Him.* **Mat. 25:31**

Q. Will He judge all men?

A. Yes. All without exception.

Q. How will He judge them?

A. The conscience of every man shall be laid open before all, and not only shall all deeds which he has ever done in his whole life upon earth be revealed, but also all the words he has spoken, and all his secret wishes and thoughts.

The Lord shall come, who will bring to light the hidden things of darkness, and will make manifest the counsels of the heart; and then shall every man have praise of God. **I Cor. 4:5**

Q. Will He then condemn us even for evil words and thoughts?

A. Yes, He will, unless we correct them by repentance, faith, and amendment of life. *I say unto you, that every idle word that men shall speak, they shall give account thereof in the day of judgement.* **Mat. 12:36**

Q. Will Jesus Christ soon come to judge the earth?

A. We do not know the day nor the hour. Therefore, we should live so as to be always ready. *The Lord is not slack concerning His promise, as some men count slackness; but is long suffering toward us, not willing that any should perish, but that all should come to repentance. But the day of the Lord will come as a thief in the night.* **II Pet. 3:9,10**

Watch, therefore, for ye know neither the day nor the hour wherein the Son of man cometh. **Mat. 25:13**

Q. What are the signs of the coming of Christ?

A. In the word of God certain signs are revealed, such as the decrease of faith and love among men, the abounding of sin and disasters, the preaching of the Gospel to all nations, and the coming of the Antichrist. **Mat. 24**

Q. What is meant by the <u>Antichrist</u>?

A. An enemy of Christ, who will strive to overthrow Christianity, but instead of doing so, shall himself come to a destructive end. **II Thess. 2:8**

Q. What is Christ's kingdom?

A. Christ's kingdom is, first, the whole world; secondly, all believers upon earth; thirdly, all the blessed in heaven.

The first is called the kingdom of nature, the second the kingdom of grace, the third the kingdom of glory.

Q. Which of these is meant when it is said in the Creed, that of Christ's Kingdom there *shall be no end*?

A. The kingdom of glory.

On the Eighth Article:

Q. In what sense is the Holy Spirit called the Lord?

A. In the same sense as the Son of God; that is, as truly God.

Q. Is it witnessed by Holy Scripture?

A. It is plain from the words spoken by the Apostle Peter to rebuke Ananias: *Why hath Satan filled thine heart, to lie to the Holy Spirit?* and further on, *Thou hast not lied unto man, but unto God.* **Acts 5:3,4**

Q. What are we to understand by this, that the Holy Spirit is called *the giver of life*?

A. That He, together with God the Father and the Son, gives life to all creatures, especially spiritual life to man. *Except a man be born of water and of the Spirit, he cannot enter into the kingdom of God.* **John 3:5**

Q. How do we know that the Holy Spirit proceeds from the Father?

A. This we know from the following words of Jesus Christ Himself: *But when the Comforter is come, whom I will send unto you from the Father, even the Spirit of truth, which proceeds from the Father, He shall testify of Me.* **John 15: 26.**

Q. Does the Doctrine of the procession of the Holy Spirit from the Father admit of any change or supplement?

A. No. First, because the Catholic Church, in this doctrine, repeats the exact words of Jesus Christ; and His words, without doubt, are a precise and perfect expression of the truth. Second, because the second Ecumenical Council, whose chief object was to establish the true doctrine concerning the Holy Spirit, has without doubt correctly set forth the same in the Creed; and the Catholic Church has acknowledged this so decidedly, that the third Ecumenical Council in its seventh canon has forbidden the composition of any new Creed.

Q. By whose authority is it stated that the Holy Spirit is equal *with the Father and the Son*, and *together* with them *is worshipped and glorified*?

A. It appears from this, that Jesus Christ commanded them to *baptize in the name of the Father, and of the Son and of the Holy Spirit.* **Mat. 28:19**

Q. Why is said in the Creed that the Holy Spirit spoke through the prophets?

A. This is said against certain heretics, who taught that the books of the Old Testament were not written by the Holy Spirit.

For prophecy came not in old time by the will of man; but holy men of God spoke as they were moved by the Holy Spirit. **II Pet. 1:12**

Q. Why then is there no mention of the Apostles in the Creed.

A. Because when the Creed was composed none doubted the inspiration of the Apostles.

Q. Was not the Holy Spirit shown forth to men in some very special manner?

A. Yes. He came down upon the Apostles in the form of fiery tongues, on the 50th day after the resurrection of Jesus Christ, the day called Pentecost.

Q. Is the Holy Spirit communicated to men even now?

A. He is communicated to all true Christians. *Know ye not that ye are the temple of God, and that the Spirit of God dwelleth in you?* **I Cor. 3:16**

Q. How may we be made partakers of the Holy Spirit?

A. Through fervent prayer, and through the Sacraments.

If ye then, being evil, know how to give good gifts unto your children how much more shall your heavenly Father give the Holy Spirit to them that ask Him? **Luke 11:13**

But after that the kindness and love of God our Savior toward man appeared, not by works of righteousness which we have done, but according to his mercy He saved us, by the washing of regeneration, and renewing of the Holy Spirit, which He shed on us abundantly through Jesus Christ our Savior. **Titus 3:4-6**

Q. What are the chief gifts of the Holy Spirit?

A. The Chief and more general are, as stated by the Prophet Isaiah, the following seven: the spirit of the fear of God, the spirit of knowledge, the spirit of might, the spirit of counsel, the spirit of understanding, the spirit of wisdom, the spirit of the Lord, or the gift of piety and inspiration and in the highest degree. **Isaiah 11:2**

On the Ninth Article:

Q. What is the Church?

A. The Church is a divinely instituted community of believers united by the catholic faith, the law of God, the hierarchy, and the Sacraments.

Q. What does it mean to *believe in the Church*?

A. It means piously to honor the true Church of Christ, and to obey her doctrine and commandments, from a conviction that grace ever abides in her, and works, teaches, and governs for salvation of men flowing from her One and only eternal Head, the Lord Jesus Christ.

Q. How can the Church, which is visible, be the object of faith, when faith, as the Apostle says, *is the evidence of things not seen*?

A. First, though the Church is visible, the grace of God which dwells in her, and in those who are sanctified in her, is not; and this is what properly constitutes the object of faith in the Church.

Second, the Church, though visible insofar as she is upon earth, and contains all right believing Christians living upon earth, still is at the same time invisible, insofar as she is also in heaven, and contains all those that have departed in true faith and holiness. **Heb. 12:22-24**

Q. How are we assured that the grace of God abides in the true Church?

A. First, that her head is Jesus Christ, God and man in one person, *full of grace and truth,* who fills His body, that is, the Church, with like grace and truth. **John 1:14,17**

Second, that He has promised His disciples the Holy Spirit to *abide with them for ever,* and that, according to this promise, the Holy Spirit appoints the pastors of the Church. **John 14:16; Eph. 1:22,23; Acts 20:28**

Q. How are we assured that the grace of God abides in the Church even to the present, and shall abide in it to the end of the world?

A. We are assured by the following words of Jesus Christ and His Apostles: *I will build my Church, and the gates of hell shall not prevail against it.* **Mat. 16:18** *I am with you always, even unto the end of the world. Amen.* **Mat. 28:20**

Unto Him, God the Father, be glory in the Church by Christ Jesus throughout all ages, world with out end Amen. **Eph. 3:21**

Q. Why is the Church one?

A. Because she is one spiritual Body, has one Head, Christ, and is given life by one Spirit of God. *There is one body and one Spirit, even as ye are called in hope of your calling in one; one Lord, one faith, one baptism; one God and Father of all.* **Eph. 4:4-6; I Cor.3:10,11; II Col.1:24,25**

Q. What duty does the unity of the Church place on us?

A. That of *endeavoring to keep the unity of the Spirit in the bond of peace.* **Eph.4:3**

Q. How does it agree with the unity of the Church that there are many separate and independent Churches, some who are called Western Rite Orthodox and others who are called Eastern Orthodox?

A. These are particular Churches, or parts of the one Catholic Church: the separateness of their visible organization does not hinder them from being spiritually great members of the one body of the Catholic Church, having one Head, Christ, and one spirit of faith and grace. This unity is expressed outwardly by unity of Creed, and by communion in Prayer and Sacraments.

Q. Is there also a unity between the church on earth and the Church in heaven?

A. There is, both by their common relation to one Head, our Lord Jesus Christ, and by mutual communion with one another.   •

Q. What means of communion does the Church on earth have with the Church in heaven?

A. The prayer of faith and love. By the offering of the same Holy Sacrifice of Christ, the faithful who belong to the Church militant upon earth, in offering their prayers to God, call upon at the same time to their aid, the Saints who belong to the Church in heaven; and these standing on the highest steps of approach to God, by their prayers of intercessions purify, strengthen, and offer before God the prayers of the faithful living upon earth, and by the will of God work graciously for and with them, either by invisible virtue, or by distinct apparitions, and in other ways.

Q. What is the basis for the rule of the Church upon earth *to invoke in prayer the Saints* of the Church in heaven?

A. The basis is Holy Tradition, the principle of which is to be seen also in Holy Scripture. For instance, when the Prophet David cries out in prayer *O Lord God of Abraham, Isaac, and of Israel our fathers,* he makes mention of Saints in aid of his prayer, exactly as now the Orthodox Catholic Church calls upon *Christ our true God, by the prayers of His most pure Mother and all His Saints.* See **1 Chron. 29:18.**

Q. Is there any testimony in Holy Scripture to the *mediatory prayer* of the Saints in heaven?

A. The Evangelist John, in the Revelation, saw in heaven an Angel, to whom *was given much incense, that he should offer it, by the prayers of all Saints, upon the golden altar which was before the throne; and the smoke of the incense ascended up by the prayers of the Saints out of the hands of the Angel before God.* **Rev. 8:3,4**

Q. Is there any testimony in Holy Scripture concerning *apparitions of Saints* from heaven?

A. The Evangelist St. Matthew relates, that after the death of our Lord Jesus Christ upon the cross, *many bodies of the Saints which slept arose, and came out of the graves after His resurrection, and went into the holy city, and appeared unto many.* **Mat. 27:52,53** And since a miracle so great could not be without some adequate purpose, we must suppose that the Saints which then arose appeared for this reason, that they might announce the descent of Jesus Christ into hell, and His triumphant resurrection.

Q. What testimonies are there to confirm us in the belief that the Saints, after their departure, work miracles through certain earthly means?

A. 1. The fourth book of Kings testifies that by touching the bones of the Prophet Elisha a dead man was raised to life. **IV Kings 13:21**

2. The Apostle Paul not only in his own immediate person administered healings and miracles, but the same was done also in his absence by handkerchiefs and aprons taken from his body. **Acts 19:12** By this example we may understand that the Saints, even after their deaths, may in like manner work through earthly means, which have been received from the holy power.

Q. Why is the Church holy?

A. Because she is sanctified by Jesus Christ through His passion, through His teaching, through His prayer, and through the Sacraments.

Christ loved the Church, and gave Himself for it; that He might sanctify it, having cleansed it with the washing of water by the word, that He might present it to Himself a glorious Church, not having spot, or wrinkle, or any such thing, but that it should be holy and without blemish. **Eph. 5:25-27**

In His prayer to God the Father for believers, Jesus Christ said among other things: *Sanctify them through Thy truth: Thy word is truth. And for their sakes I Sanctify Myself, that they also may be sanctified in truth.* **John 17:17-19**

Q. How is the Church holy, when she has in her body many sinners?

A. Men who sin, but purify themselves by true repentance, do not hinder the Church from being holy, but impenitent sinners, either by the visible act of Church authority, or by the invisible judgement of God, are cut off from the body of the Church: and so she is with respect to these also kept holy. *Put away from among yourselves that wicked person.* **I Cor. 5:13** *Nevertheless the foundation of God stands sure, having this seal, the Lord knows them that are His. and let every one that calls on the name of the Lord depart from iniquity.* **II Tim. 2:19**

Q. Why is the Church called <u>Catholic</u>?

A. Because she is not limited to any place, nor time, nor people, but contains true believers of all places, times, and peoples; hence, she is universal.

The Apostle Paul says that *the word of the gospel is in all the world; and brings forth fruit.* **Coloss. 1:5,6** and that in the Christian Church there *is neither Greek nor Jew, circumcision nor uncircumcision, barbarian nor Scythian, bond nor free: but Christ is all, and in all.* **ib. 3:11**

They which be of faith are blessed with faithful Abraham. **Gal. 3:9**

Q. What great privilege has the Catholic Church been given?

A. She alone has the sublime promises *that the gates of hell shall not prevail against her;* that the Lord shall *be with her even to the end of the world;* that in her shall abide *the glory of God in Jesus Christ throughout all generations for ever;* and consequently that she shall never apostatize from the faith, nor sin against the truth of the faith, of fall into error.

Q. If the Catholic Church contains all true believers in the World, must we not acknowledge it to be necessary for salvation, that every believer should belong to her?

A. Yes. Since Jesus Christ, in the words of St. Paul, *is the Head of the Church, and He is the Saviour of the Body;* it follows that in order to have a participation in His salvation, we must be members of His Body, that is, of the Catholic Church. **Ephes. 5:23**

The Apostle Peter writes that *baptism saves us* after the figure of the *the ark of Noah*. All who were saved from the great flood were saved only in the ark; so all who obtain everlasting salvation, obtain it only in the one Catholic Church.

Q. Why is the Church called <u>Apostolic</u>?

A. Because she has from the Apostles without breakage or change both her doctrine and the succession of the gifts of the Holy Spirit, through the laying on of consecrated hands. **Ephes. 2:19,20**

Q. What does the Creed teach us, when she calls the Church Apostolic?

A. It teaches us to hold fast the Apostolic doctrine and tradition, and cast out such doctrine and such teachers, as are not in conformity with the doctrine of the Apostles. **II Thess. 2:15; Titus 3:10; Titus 1:10,11; Mat. 18:17**

Q. What Ecclesiastical Institution is there through which the succession of the Apostolic ministry is preserved?

A. The Hierarchy of Bishops, Priest, and Deacons.

Q. Where does the Hierarchy of the Orthodox Catholic Church have its beginnings?

A. From Jesus Christ Himself, and from the descent of the Holy Spirit on the Apostles; from which time it has continued in unbroken succession, through the laying on of hands, in the sacrament of Holy Orders.

And He gave some, Apostles, and some, Prophets; and some, Evangelists; and some, Pastors and Teachers; for the perfecting of the Saints, for the work of the ministry, for the edifying of the Body of Christ. **Eph. 4:11,12**

Q. What is the highest authority in the Catholic Church?

A. An Ecumenical Council.

Q. What is the highest authority of sections of the Catholic Church?

A. An Archbishop and the Synod.

Q. Under what ecclesiastical authority are dioceses and vicariates?

A. Under the authority of Bishops.

Q. If anyone desires to fulfill his duty of obedience to the Church, how may he learn what she requires of her children?

A. This may be learned from Holy Scripture, from the canons of the Holy Apostles, the seven Holy Ecumenical and various Provincial Councils, and the Holy Fathers, and from the Books of Ecclesiastical Canons.

On the Tenth Article:

Q. Why does the Creed mention Baptism?

A. Because faith is sealed by Baptism and the other Sacraments.

Q. What is a Sacrament?

A. A Sacrament is a holy act, through which grace, the saving power of God, works supernaturally upon man, and is instituted by Christ.

Q. How many Sacraments are there?

A. Seven: 1) Baptism; 2) Confirmation/Chrismation; 3) Holy Eucharist; 4) Penance; 5) Holy orders; 6) Matrimony; 7) Anointing of the Sick.

Q. What virtue is there in each of these Sacraments?

A.1. In Baptism man is born to a new spiritual life.

2. In confirmation he receives the grace of spiritual growth and strength, and is made a member of the universal priesthood of all believers.

3. In the Communion, or Holy Eucharist, he is spiritually fed upon the Body and Blood of Christ.

4. In Penance he is cleansed of spiritual diseases, that is, of sin.

5. In Holy Orders he receives grace spiritually to regenerate, feed, and nurture others, by doctrine and Sacraments.

6. In Matrimony he receives a grace sanctifying the married life, and the natural procreation and nurture of children.

7. In Anointing of the Sick he has medicine even for bodily diseases, in that he is healed of spiritual ones.

Q. But why does the Creed not mention all these Sacraments, instead of mentioning Baptism only?

A. Because Baptism was the subject of a question, whether some people, as heretics, ought not to be rebaptized; and this required a decision, which so came to be put into the Creed.

On Baptism:

Q. What is baptism?

A. Baptism is a Sacrament in which a believer having his body plunged three times in water, or water poured three times, in the name of God the Father, the Son, and the Holy Spirit, dies to the life of sin, both original and actual, and is born again of the Holy Spirit to a life spiritual and holy. *Except a man be born of water and of the Spirit, he cannot enter into the kingdom of God.* **John 3:5**

Q. When and how did Baptism begin?

A. First, *John baptized with the baptism of repentance, saying unto the people that they should believe on Him which should come after him, that is, on Christ Jesus.* **Acts 19:4** Afterwards, Jesus Christ by His own example sanctified Baptism when He received it from John. Finally, after His resurrection He gave the Apostles the solemn commandment: *Go ye and teach all nations, baptizing them in the name of the Father, and of the Son, and of the Holy Spirit.* **Mat.28:19**

Q. What is most essential in the administration of Baptism?

A. Threefold immersion in water, or pouring of water, in the name of the Father, and of the Son, and of the Holy Spirit.

Q. What is required of those who seek to be baptized?

A. Repentance, and faith; which is why before Baptism they recite the Creed. *Repent, and be baptized every one of you in the name of Christ Jesus for the remission of sins, and ye shall receive the gift of the Holy Spirit.* **Acts 2:38**

He that believes and is baptized, shall be saved. **Mark 16:16**

Q. But why then are children baptized?

A. Because of the faith of their parents and sponsors, who are also bound to teach them the faith as soon as they are of an age to learn.

Q. How can you show from Holy Scripture that we ought to baptize infants?

A. In the time of the Old Testament infants were circumcised when eight days old; but Baptism in the New Testament takes the place of circumcision; consequently infants should also be baptized. *Suffer the little Children.*

Q. Where in Scripture does it state that Baptism takes the place of circumcision?

A. From the following words of the Apostle Paul to believers: *Ye are circumcised with the circumcision made without hands, in putting off the body of the sins of the flesh, by the circumcision of Christ, buried with Him in Baptism.* **Coloss. 2:11,12**

Q. Why are there sponsors at Baptism?

A. In order that they may stand as witnesses before the Church for the faith of the baptized, and after Baptism, if need be, assume the religious education of the child if the parents neglect to do so.

Q. Why before baptizing do we use exorcism?

A. To drive away the devil, who since Adam's fall has had power over men. The Apostle Paul says that all men, without grace, *walk according to the course of this world, according to the prince of the power of the air, the spirit that now works in the children of disobedience.* **Ephes. 2:2**

Q. What name bears the force of exorcism?

A. The name of Jesus Christ, invoked with prayer and faith. Jesus Christ gave to believers this promise. *In My name shall they cast out devils.* **Mark 16:17**

Q. What force does the sign of the cross have on this and other occasions?

A. What the name of Jesus Christ crucified is when pronounced with faith by motion of the lips, the same is true concerning the sign of the cross when made with faith by motion of the hand, or represented in any other way.

Q. When did the sign of the cross originate?

A. From the times of the Apostles.

Q. What does the white garment, which is put on after Baptism symbolize?

A. The purity of the soul and of the Christian life.

Q. Why do they often place a small cross upon the baptized?

A. As a visible expression and continual remembrance of Christ's command: *If any man will come after me. let him deny himself, and take up his cross, and follow Me.* **Mat. 16:24**

Q. What is symbolized by giving the baptized a candle?

A. Spiritual joy joined with spiritual illumination.

Q. How is this to be understood, that in the Creed we confess one Baptism?

A. That Baptism cannot be repeated.

Q. Why cannot Baptism be repeated?

A. Baptism is spiritual birth: a man is born but once; therefor, he is also baptized but once.

Q. What is the state of those who sin after Baptism?

A. That they are more guilty of their sins than the unbaptized, since they had from God special help to do well, and have cast it away.

For if after they have escaped the pollutions of the world through the knowledge of the Lord and Saviour Jesus Christ, they are again entangled therein and overcome, the latter end is worse with them that the beginning. **II Pet. 2:20**

Q. Is there another way for those who sin after Baptism to obtain pardon?

A. There is; through the Sacrament of Penance.

On Confirmation:

Q. What is Confirmation, or Chrismation?

A. Confirmation/Chrismation, is a Sacrament in which the baptized believer, being anointed with holy chrism in the name of the Holy Spirit, as well as having hands laid on him, receives the gifts of the Holy Spirit for growth and strength in spiritual life, and full membership in the universal priesthood of the laity. **I John 2:20-27; 2 Cor. 1: 21,22**

Q. Is the outward form of anointing with chrism mentioned in Holy Scripture?

A. It may well be supposed that the words of St. John refer to a visible as well as to an inward anointing; but it is more certain that the Apostles, for imparting to the baptized the gifts of the Holy Spirit, used *imposition of hands.* **Acts 7:14-16**

Q. What is to be said of the holy chrism?

A. That its consecration is reserved to the hands of the Hierarchy, as successors of the Apostles, who used the laying on of their own hands to communicate the gifts of the Holy Spirit.

Q. What is signified by anointing the forehead?

A. The sanctification of the mind, which governs the whole person.

On the Holy Eucharist:

Q. What is the Holy Eucharist?

A. The Holy Eucharist is a Sacrament in which the believer, under the forms of bread and wine, partakes of the true Body and Blood of Christ unto everlasting life.

Q. How was this Sacrament instituted?

A. Jesus Christ immediately before His passion consecrated it for the first time, showing in it by anticipation a sign of His sufferings for our salvation. After having administered it to the Apostles, He gave them at the same time the power to perpetuate this Sacrament.

Q. What is to be said of the Sacrament of the Holy Eucharist in regard to Divine Service in the Church?

A. That it forms the chief and most essential part of Divine Service.

Q. What is the name of that Service, in which the Sacrament of the Holy Eucharist is consecrated?

A. The Liturgy or the Mass.

Q. What does the word *Liturgy* mean?

A. Common service.

Q. What does the word *Mass* mean?

A. Dismissal, taken from the end of the liturgy, where the Church is sent forth to bear Christ into the world.

Q. What is to be noted about the place where the Liturgy normally is celebrated?

A. It must normally be celebrated in a Church which the Bishop has approved.

Q. What does the word Church mean?

A. An assembly.

Q. Why is the table on which the Liturgy or Mass is celebrated called an altar?

A. Because on it Jesus Christ, as King, is mystically present and offered.

Q. What are the two major divisions of the Mass?

A. First, the Mass of the Catechumens, or instructional part; second, the Mass of the Faithful. or the Eucharist proper.

Q. What are the divisions of the Mass of the Catechumens?

A. 1. Confession of sin.
2. Praise.
3. Prayer.
4. Epistle.
5. Gospel.
6. Sermon (Homily)

Q. What are the major Divisions of the Mass of the Faithful?

A. 1. Offering of bread and wine.
2. The Eucharistic Prayer or Canon.
3. The Invocation of the Holy Spirit and the Words of Institution. **Mat. 26:26-28**
4. Prayers for the Living and the Dead.
5. The Lord's Prayer.
6. Breaking of the Sacred Bread.
7. The Communion Rite.
8. The Thanksgiving.
9. The Blessing and Dismissal.

Q. Why is the bread used in the Mass sometimes called the Lamb or Host?

A. Because it is the figure of Jesus Christ suffering, as was in the Old Testament *the Paschal Lamb,* and because He is the Victim or Host of the Sacrifice.

Q. What was the Paschal Lamb?

A. The lamb which the Israelites, by God's command, killed and ate in memory of their deliverance from destruction in Egypt; it was offered in sacrifice.

Q. Why is the wine for the Mass or Liturgy mixed with water?

A. Because the whole of this celebration is ordered so as to show forth the sufferings of Christ; and when He suffered there flowed from His pierced side blood and water.

Q. What happens at the moment of Invocation—Consecration in the Mass?

A. At the moment of this act, the bread and wine are changed, or transubstantiated, into the Body and Blood of Christ.

Q. How are we to understand the word *transubstantiation*?

A. That the bread truly, really, and substantially becomes the true Body of the Lord, and the wine the true Blood of the Lord. It is a mystery which the mind cannot understand, but it is received in faith.

Q. What is required of everyone who approaches the Sacrament of Holy Communion?

A. Each one is required to examine his conscience before God, to confess one's sins, to seek absolution, and to fast according to the laws of the Church. **I Cor. 11:28,29**

Q. What benefit does one receive who communicates in the Body and Blood of Christ?

A. He is in the closest manner united to Jesus Christ Himself, and, in Him, is made partaker of everlasting life. **John 6:56; 5:54**

Q. Should we communicate often in the Holy Mysteries of Christ.

A. The primitive Christians communicated every Lord's Day. The Church calls on all who would live religiously to confess before their heavenly Father, and communicate in the Body and Blood of Christ whenever they attend Mass or are ill, but requires all without exception to receive It at least once a year during the Easter time.

Q. What part do they have in the Liturgy or the Mass who only hear it without receiving Holy Communion.

A. They may and should take part of the Liturgy by prayer and faith, and especially by continual remembrance of our Lord Jesus Christ, who expressly has commanded us *to do this in remembrance of Him.* **Luke 22:19**

Q. What should we remember at the time in the Liturgy when the Gospel is proclaimed?

A. That Jesus Christ is present to preach the Gospel. Therefore, we should have the same attention and reverence, as if we saw and heard Jesus Christ in the flesh.

Q. What should we remember at the time in the Liturgy when the bread and wine are offered?

A. That Jesus Christ is going to suffer voluntarily as a victim to the slaughter.

Q. What should we remember at the moment of the consecration of the bread and wine?

A. The Last Supper of Jesus Christ himself with His Apostles, and also His suffering, death, burial, resurrection, Ascension, and that He will come again to His people.

Q. Will the Sacrament of the Holy Eucharist continue forever in the true Church of Christ?

A. Yes, it will continue until Christ's coming again, as the Apostle Paul testified: *For as often as ye eat this bread, and drink this cup, ye do show forth the Lord's death, till He come.* **I Cor. 11:26**

On the Sacrament of Penance:

Q. What is Penance?

A. Penance is a Sacrament in which he who confesses receives, through the absolution of the Priest, forgiveness of his sins by Jesus Christ Himself. **Mark 1:4,5; Mat. 18:18; John 20:22,23**

Q. What is required of the Penitent.

A. Contrition for his sins, with full purpose of amendment of life, faith in Jesus Christ, and hope in His mercy. **II Cor. 7:10; Ezek. 33:19**

Q. In what ways can we prepare for the Sacrament?

A. By fasting, prayer, examination of conscience, and by penance.

Q. What is meant by the term *penance?*

A. The word means contrition. See **2 Cor. 2:6.**

On the Sacrament of Holy Orders:

Q. What is Holy Orders?

A. Holy Orders is a Sacrament in which the Holy Spirit, through the laying on of the bishop's hands, ordains those who are chosen to administer the sacraments, and to feed the flock of Christ. *Let a man so account of us, as of the ministers of Christ, and stewards of the Mysteries of God.* **I Cor. 4:1**

Take heed therefore unto yourselves, and to all the flock, over which the Holy Spirit has made you overseers, to feed the Church of God, which He has purchased with His own Blood. **Acts 20:28**

Q. What does it mean to feed the Church?

A. It means to instruct the people in faith, piety, and good works.

Q. How many necessary degrees are there of Holy Orders?

A. Three: those of Bishop, Priest, and Deacon.

Q. What difference is there between them?

A. The Deacon serves at the altar; the Priest administers the Sacraments in dependence upon the Bishop; the Bishop not only administers the Sacraments himself, but has power also to ordain to others, by laying on of his hands, the office of Deacon, Priest, and Bishop.

Of the Episcopal power the Apostle Paul writes to Titus: *For this cause I Left thee in Crete, that thou should set in order the things that are wanting. and ordain elders in every city.* **Titus 1:5**

And to Timothy: *Lay hands suddenly on no man.* **I Tim. 5:22**

On the Sacrament of Matrimony:

Q. What is Matrimony?

A. Matrimony is a Sacrament in which, on the free promise of the man and woman before the Priest and the Church to be true to each other, their union is blessed to be an image of Christ's union with the Church, and grace is asked for them to live together in love and honesty, and for the procreation and Christian upbringing of children.

Q. From what source do we know that Matrimony is a Sacrament?

A. From the following words of the Apostle Paul: *A man shall leave his father and mother, and shall be joined unto his wife, and they two shall be one flesh. This mystery is great; but I speak concerning Christ and the Church.* **Eph. 5:31,32**

Q. Is it the duty of all to marry?

A. No. Virginity is another way in which to serve Christ. **Mat. 19:11,12; 1 Cor: 7:8,9,32,33,38**

On the Sacrament of Anointing of the Sick:

Q. What is Anointing of the Sick?

A. Anointing of the Sick is a Sacrament in which, while the body is anointed with oil, God's grace is invoked on the sick person to heal him of spiritual and bodily illnesses.

Q. What is the origin in Scripture of this Sacrament?

A. From the Apostles, who having received power from Jesus Christ, *anointed with oil many that were sick, and healed them.* **Mark 6:13**

The Apostles left this Sacrament to the Priests of the Church, as is evident from the following words of the Apostle James: *Is any sick among you? Let him call for the Elders of the Church; and let them pray over him, anointing him with oil in the name of the Lord: and the prayer of faith shall save the sick, and the Lord shall raise him up: and if he have committed sins, they shall be forgiven him.* **James 5:14,15**

On the Eleventh Article:

Q. What is the *resurrection of the dead.* which, in the words of the Creed, we *look for* or expect?

A. An act of the almighty power of God, by which the bodies of dead men, being reunited to their souls, shall return to life, and shall be made glorious and immortal. *It is sown a natural body, it is raised a spiritual body.* **I Cor. 15:44**

For this corruptible must put on incorruption and mortal must put on immortality. **Ib. 53.**

Q. How shall the body rise again after it has decomposed in the ground?

A. Since God formed the body from the ground originally, He can equally restore it after it has perished in the ground. The Apostle Paul illustrates this by the analogy of a grain of seed, which decomposes in the earth, but from which there springs up afterwards a plant of tree. *That which thou sows in not quickened except it die.* **I Cor. 15:36**

Q. Shall all strictly speaking rise again?

A. All, without exception, that have died; but they, who at the time of the general resurrection shall still be alive, shall have their present mortal bodies changed in a moment, so as to become spiritual and immortal.

We shall not all sleep, but we shall all be changed, in a moment, in the twinkling of an eye, at the last trump; for the trumpet shall sound, and the dead shall be raised incorruptible, and we shall be changed. **I Cor. 15:36**

Q. When shall the resurrection of the dead be?

A. At the end of the visible world.

Q. Shall the world then too come to an end?

A. Yes; this corruptible world shall come to an end, and shall be transformed into an incorruptible one. *Because the creature itself also shall be delivered from the bondage of corruption into the glorious liberty of the children of God.* **Rom. 8:21**

Nevertheless we, according to His promise, look for new heavens and a new earth, wherein dwells righteousness. **II Pet. 3:13**

Q. How shall the world be transformed?

A. By fire. *The heavens and the earth, which are not, by the same,* that is by God's word, *are kept in store, reserved unto fire against the day of judgement and perdition of ungodly men.* **II Pet. 3:7**

Q. In what state are the souls of the dead until the general resurrection?

A. The souls of the righteous are in light and rest, with a foretaste of eternal happiness; but the souls of the wicked are in a state the reverse of this.

Q. Why may we not ascribe to the souls of the saved perfect happiness immediately after death?

A. Because it is ordained that the perfect retribution according to works shall be received by the perfect man, after the resurrection of the body and God's last judgement.

The Apostle Paul says: *Hence forth there is laid up for me a crown of righteousness, which the Lord, the righteous Judge, shall give me at that day: and not to me only, but unto all them also that love His appearing.* **II Tim. 4:8**

And again; *We must all appear before the Judgement-seat of Christ; that everyone may receive the things done in his body, according to what He has done, whether it be good or bad.* **II Cor. 5:10**

Q. Why do we speak of the souls of the saved as having a taste of bliss before the last judgement?

A. Jesus Christ Himself has said in a parable that Lazarus was immediately after death carried into Abraham's bosom. **Luke 16:22**

Q. Is this foretaste of bliss joined with a sight of Christ's own countenance?

A. It is so with the Saints, as we are given to understand by the Apostle Paul, who *had a desire to depart, and to be with Christ.* **Philipp. 1:23**

Q. What is to be said of such souls who have departed with faith, but without having had time to bring forth fruits worthy of repentance?

A. That they may be aided towards the attainment of a blessed resurrection by prayers offered in their behalf, especially such as are offered in union with the Bloodless Sacrifice of the Body and Blood of Christ, and by works of mercy done in faith for their memory.

Q. On what is this doctrine grounded?

A. On the constant tradition of the Catholic Church; the source of which may be seen even in the Church of the Old Testament. Judas Maccabeus offered sacrifice for his men who had died. **II Macc. 12:43** Prayer for the departed has ever formed a fixed part of the Liturgy of the Apostle James.

On the Twelfth Article:

Q. What is *the life of the world to come*?

A. The life that shall be after the resurrection of the dead and the general judgement of Christ.

Q. What kind of life shall this be?

A. For those who believe, who love God, and do what is good, it shall be a life of happiness. *It does not yet appear what we shall be.* **I John 3:2**

I knew a man in Christ, says the Apostle Paul, *who was caught up into Paradise, and heard unspeakable words, which it is not lawful for a man to utter.* **II Cor.12:2,4**

Q. What is the object of this great happiness?

A. The contemplation of God in light and glory, and union with Him. *For now we see through a glass darkly, but then face to face: now I know in part, but then shall I know, even as also I am known.* **I Cor. 13:12**

Then shall the righteous shine forth as the sun, in the kingdom of their Father. **Mat. 13:43**

God shall be all in all. **I Cor. 15:28**

Q. Shall the body also share in the happiness of the soul?

A. Yes; it, too, shall be glorified with the light of God, as Christ's body was at His Transfiguration on Mount Tabor. *It is sown in dishonor, it is raised in glory.* **I Cor. 15:43**

As we have borne the image of the earthy, that is of Adam, *we shall also bear the image of the heavenly.* **ib. 49**

Q. Will all be equally happy?

A. No. There will be different degrees of happiness, in proportion to the faith, love, and good works carried out in this life.

There is one glory of the sun, and another glory of the moon, and another glory of the stars: for one star differs from another star in glory. So also is the resurrection of the dead. **I Cor. 15:41,42**

Q. But what will be the lot of unbelievers and transgressors?

A. They will be given over to everlasting death, that is, to everlasting fire, to everlasting torment, with the devils. *Whosoever was not found written in the book of life, was cast into the lake of fire.* **Rev. 20:15**

That is the second death. **Rev. 20:14**

Depart from Me, ye cursed, into everlasting fire, prepared for the devil and his angels. **Mat. 25:41**

And these shall go away into everlasting punishment, but the righteous into life eternal. **ib. 46**

It is better for thee to enter into the kingdom of God with one eye, that having two eyes to be cast into hell fire; where their worm dies not, and the fire is not quenched. **Mark 9:47,48**

Q. Why will such severity be used with sinners?

A. Not because God willed them to perish, but they of their own will *perish, because they receive not the love of the truth, that they might be saved.* **II Thess. 2:10**

Q. Of what benefit will it be for us to meditate on death, on the resurrection, on the last judgement, on everlasting happiness, and on everlasting torment?

A. These meditations will assist us to abstain from sin, and to uplift our affections from earthly things; they will console us for the absence or loss of earthly goods, encourage us to keep our souls and bodies pure, to live for God, and for eternity.

THE SECOND PART: ON HOPE

Definition of Christian Hope:

Q. What is Christian Hope?

A. The resting of the heart on God, with full trust that He always cares for our salvation, and will give us the happiness He has promised.

Q. What is the Scriptural source of Christian Hope?

A. The Lord Jesus is our hope, or the source of our hope. **I Tim. 1:1** *Hope to the end for the grace that is to be brought unto you by the revelation of Jesus Christ.* **I Pet. 1:13**

Q. What are the means for attaining to a saving hope?

A. The means to this are: first, prayer: second, the Beatitudes, and their practice.

On Prayer:

Q. Is there any testimony of God's word, that prayer is a means for attaining a saving hope?

A. Jesus Christ Himself joins the hope of receiving our desire with prayer: *Whatsoever ye shall ask of the Father in My name, that will I do, that the Father may be glorified in the Son.* **John 14:13**

Q. What is prayer?

A. The lifting up of man's mind and heart and soul to God.

Q. What should Christians do when we they lift up our minds and hearts and souls to God?

A. First, we should glorify Him for His divine perfection; second, give thanks to Him for his mercies; third, seek His forgiveness; and fourth, ask God for what we need, So there are four chief forms of prayer: <u>Praise</u>, <u>Thanksgiving</u>, <u>Contrition</u>, and <u>Petition</u>.

Q. Can a man pray without words?

A. He can; in mind and heart. An example of this may be seen in Moses before the passage through the Red Sea. **Exod. 15:15**

On the Lord's Prayer:

Q. Is there a prayer which may be termed the common Christian prayer, and pattern of all prayers?

A. Such is the Lord's Prayer.

Q. What is the Lord's Prayer?

A. A prayer which our Lord Jesus Christ taught the Apostles, and which they delivered to all believers:

Q. How may we divide the Lord's Prayer?

A. Into the invocation and seven petitions.
"Our Father, Who art in heaven;
1. Hallowed be Thy name;
2. Thy kingdom come;
3. Thy will be done, on earth as it is in heaven.
4. Give us this day our daily bread,
5. And for give us our trespasses, as we for give those who trespass against us.
6. And lead us not into temptation;
7. But deliver us from evil. Amen."

On the Invocation:

Q. How are we able to call God *Father*?

A. By faith in Jesus Christ, and by the grace of regeneration. *As many as received Him, to them gave He power to become sons of God, even to them that believe on His name; which were born, not of blood, nor of the will of the flesh, nor of the will of man, but God.* **John 1:12,13**

Q. Why do we say *Our Father* even when we pray alone?

A. Because Christian charity requires us to call upon God, and ask good things of Him, for all our brethren, no less than for ourselves.

Q. Why in the invocation do we say, *Who art in heaven*?

A. That entering into prayer we may leave everything earthly and corruptible and raise our minds and hearts to what is heavenly, everlasting, and Divine.

On the First Petition:

Q. Is God's Name holy?

A. *Holy is His Name.* **Luke 1:49**

Q. How then can it yet be made holy?

A. It may be made holy in men; that is, His eternal holiness may be made known in them. **Mat. 5:16**

On the Second Petition:

Q. What is the kingdom of God, spoken of in the second petition of the Lord's Prayer?

A. The kingdom of grace, which, as St. Paul says, is *righteousness, and peace, and joy in the Holy Spirit.* **Rom. 14:17**

Q. Has not this kingdom come already?

A. To some it has not come in its full sense; while to others it has not yet come at all, inasmuch as *sin still reigns in their mortal bodies, that they should obey it in the lusts thereof.* **Rom. 7:12**

Q. How does it come?

A. Secretly and inwardly. *The kingdom of God comes not with observation; for behold, the kingdom of God is within you.* **Luke 17:20,21**

Q. May not the Christian ask for something further under the name of God's kingdom?

A. He may ask for the kingdom of glory, that is, for the perfect bliss of the faithful. *Having a desire to depart, and be with Christ.* **Philipp. 1:23**

On the Third Petition:

Q. What does the petition. *Thy will be done* mean?

A. In this petition we ask God, that all we do, and all that happens to us may be not as we will, but as pleases Him.

Q. Why should we ask this favor?

A. Because we often err in our wishes; but God unerringly, and incomparably more than we ourselves, wishes for us all that is good, and is ever ready to bestow it, unless He be prevented by our willingness and stubbornness.

Unto Him that is able to do exceeding abundantly above all that we ask or think, according to the power that works in us, unto Him be glory in the Church. **Ephes. 3:20,21**

Q. Why do we ask that God's will be done in earth *as in heaven*?

A. Because in heaven the Holy Angels and Saints in bliss, all without exception, always, and in all things, do God's will.

On the Fourth Petition:

Q. What is *our daily bread*?

A. The bread which we need in order to subsist or live.

Q. With what thoughts should we ask God for this bread?

A. Agreeably with the instruction of Our Lord Jesus Christ, we should ask no more than bread for subsistence; that is, necessary food, and such clothing and shelter as is likewise necessary for life; but whatever is beyond this, and serves not so much for necessity as for gratification, we should leave to the will of God; and if it be given, return thanks to Him; if it be not given, we should be content without it.

Q. Why are we directed to ask for bread for subsistence only for this day?

A. That we may not be too anxious about the future, trusting God. *Take therefore no thought for the morrow, for the morrow shall take thought for the things of itself: sufficient unto the day is the evil thereof.* **Mat. 6:34**

For your heavenly Father knows that ye have need of all these things. **ib. 32**

Q. May we not ask for something further under the name of bread for subsistence?

A. Since man is made of both bodily and a spiritual substance, and the substance of the soul far excels that of the body, we may and should seek for the soul also that bread of subsistence, without which the inward man must perish of hunger.

Q. What is the bread of subsistence for the soul?

A. The Word of God, and the Body and Blood of Christ. *Man shall not live by bread alone, but by every word that proceeds out of the mouth of God.* **Matt 4:4**

My Flesh is meat indeed, and my Blood is drink indeed. **John 6:55**

On the Fifth Petition:

Q. What is meant in the Lord's Prayer by *our trespasses*?

A. Our sins.

Q. Why are our sins called trespasses?

A. Because we, having received all from God, ought to render all back to Him, that is subject all to His will and law.

Q. Who are *those who trespass against us*?

A. People who have not rendered us that which they owed us by the law of God; as, for instance, have not shown us love, but malice.

Q. If God is just, how can we be forgiven our trespasses?

A. Through the mediation of Jesus Christ. *For there is one God, and one Mediator between God and man, the man Jesus Christ, who gave himself ransom for all.* **I Tim. 2:5,6**

Q. What will be the consequence if we ask God to forgive us our sins without ourselves forgiving others?

A. In that case we shall not be forgiven.

For if ye forgive men their trespasses, your heavenly Father will also forgive you; but if you forgive not men their trespasses, neither will your Father forgive you your trespasses. **Mat. 6:14,15**

Q. Why will God not forgive us if we do not forgive others?

A. Because we show ourselves unrepentant, and so alienate from us God's goodness and mercy.

Q. What disposition then must we have when we pray *we forgive those who trespass against us.*

A. These words absolutely require that when we pray we should bear no malice nor hatred, but be in peace and charity with all men.

Therefore if thou bring thy gift to the altar, and there remember that thy brother has aught against thee, leave there thy gift before the altar, and go thy way; first be reconciled to thy brother, and then come and offer thy gift. **Mat. 5:23,24**

Q. But what am I to do if I cannot readily find him who holds malice toward me, or if he is unwilling to be reconciled?

A. In such a case it is enough to be reconciled with him in heart, before the eyes of the all-seeing God. *If it be possible, as much as lies in you, live peaceably with all men.* **Rom. 12:18**

On the Sixth Petition:

Q. What is meant in the Lord's Prayer by *temptation?*

A. Any circumstance in which there is imminent danger of losing the faith, or falling into great sin.

Q. What are the sources of temptation?

A. From our flesh, from the world, or other people, and from the devil.

Q. What do we ask in these words of the prayer, *Lead us not into temptation?*

A. That God guide us during times of temptation in the keeping of His laws.

On the Seventh Petition:

Q. What do we ask in these words of the prayer, *deliver us from evil*?

A. We ask for deliverance from all evil that can reach us in the world, which since the fall *lies in wickedness*; **I John 5:19**; but especially from the evil of sin, and from the evil temptations of the spirit of evil, which is the devil.

Q. What does the word *Amen* mean?

A. It means <u>so be it</u>.

Q. Why is this word added to the end of prayers?

A. To signify that we offer the prayer in faith, and with out doubting, as we are taught to do by the Apostle James in his Epistle, **1:6.**

On the Doctrine of Blessedness:

Q. What must we join with prayer, in order to be grounded in the hope of salvation and blessedness?

A. Our own works for the attainment of blessedness. Of the point the Lord Himself says: *Why call ye Me Lord, Lord, and do not the things which I say?* **Luke 6:46**

Not every one that says unto Me Lord, Lord shall enter into the kingdom of heaven, but he that does the will of my Father, which is in heaven. **Mat. 7:21**

Q. What doctrine may we take as our guide in these works?

A. The doctrine of our Lord Jesus Christ, which is briefly set forth in His Beatitudes, or sentences on blessedness.

Q. How many such sentences are there?

A. The Following nine:

1. Blessed are the poor in spirit: for theirs is the kingdom of Heaven.
2. Blessed are they that mourn: for they shall be comforted.
3. Blessed are the meek: for they shall inherit the earth.

4. Blessed are they which hunger and thirst after righteousness: for they shall be filled.

5. Blessed are the merciful: for they shall obtain mercy.

6. Blessed are the pure in heart: for they shall see God.

7. Blessed are the peacemakers: for they shall be called the children of God.

8. Blessed are they that are persecuted for righteousness' sake: for theirs is the kingdom of heaven.

9. Blessed are ye, when men shall revile you, and persecute you, and shall say all manner of evil against you falsely, for My sake. Rejoice, and be exceedingly glad: for great is your reward in heaven. **Mat. 5:3-12**

Q. What is to be observed of all these Beatitudes?

A. That the Lord proposed in these sentences a doctrine for the attainment of blessedness, as is expressly said in the Gospel; *He opened His mouth, and taught*; but, being meek and lowly of heart, He proposed His doctrine not in the form of a commandment, but a blessing to those, who should of their own free will receive and fulfill it. Consequently in each sentence or Beatitude we must consider, first, the doctrine or precept, and second, the blessing or promise of reward.

On the First Beatitude:

Q. What is the Lord's first precept of blessedness?

A. They who would be blessed must be *poor in spirit.*

Q. What does it mean to be *poor in spirit*?

A. It is to have a spiritual conviction that we have nothing of our own, nothing but what God bestows upon us, and that we can do nothing good without God's help and grace, thus counting ourselves as nothing, and in all things, throwing ourselves upon the mercy of God: in brief, as St. John Chrysostom explains it, *spiritual poverty is humility.* **Hom. on Mat. 15**

Q. Can the rich too be poor in spirit?

A. Most certainly, if they in a manner that shows that visible riches are corruptible and soon pass away, and can never compensate for the want of spiritual goods. *What is a man profited, if he gain the whole world, and lose his own soul? Or what shall a man give in exchange for his soul?* **Mat. 16:26**

Q. Can bodily poverty aid in spiritual perfection?

A. It can if the Christian chooses it voluntarily for God's sake. Of this, Jesus Christ Himself said to the rich man: *If thou will be perfect, go, sell that thou has, and give to the poor, and thou shalt have treasure in heaven; and come follow Me.* Mat. 19:21

Q. What does our Lord promise to the poor in spirit?

A. The kingdom of heaven.

Q. How is the kingdom of heaven theirs?

A. In the present life inwardly through faith and hope; but in the life to come perfectly, by their being made partakers of everlasting blessedness.

On the Second Beatitude:

Q. What is the Lord's second precept for blessedness?

A. They who would be blessed must mourn.

Q. What is meant in this precept by the word *mourn*?

A. Sorrow and change of heart for unworthy serving the Lord, or even rather for deserving His anger by our sins. *For godly sorrow works repentance unto salvation not to be repented of; but the sorrow of this world works death.* **II Cor. 7:10**

Q. What special promise does the Lord make to mourners?

A. They *shall be comforted.*

Q. What comfort is here to be understood?

A. That of grace, consisting in the pardon of sins and in peace of conscience.

Q. Why is this promise joined with a precept for mourning?

A. In order that sorrow for sin may not reach to despair.

On the Third Beatitude:

Q. What is the Lord's third precept of blessedness?

A. They who would be blessed must be meek.

Q. What is meekness?

A. A quiet attitude of spirit, joined with the care neither to offend any man, nor be offended at anything.

Q. What are the special effects of Christian meekness?

A. That we never speak against God, nor against men, nor give way to anger.

Q. What is promised by the Lord to the meek?

A. That *they shall inherit the earth.*

Q. How are we to understand this promise?

A As regards Christ's followers generally it is a prediction which is being literally fulfilled; for the ever-meek Christians instead of being destroyed by the anger of unbelievers, will inherit the universe. But the further sense of the promise, as regards Christians both generally and individually, is this that they shall receive an inheritance, as the Psalmist says, *in the land of the living*: that is, where men live and never die; in other words, that they shall receive everlasting blessedness. *See* **Psalm 27:15.**

On the Fourth Beatitude:

Q. What is the Lord's fourth precept for blessedness?

A. They who would be blessed must *hunger and thirst after righteousness.*

Q. What is meant here by the word *righteousness*?

A. Though this word may well stand for every virtue, which the Christian ought to desire, yet we should especially understand it to mean the justification of guilty man through grace and faith in Jesus Christ. **Dan. 9:24**

The Apostle Paul speaks thus: *The righteousness of God which is by faith of Jesus Christ unto all, and upon all them that believe: for there is no difference: for all have sinned, and come short of the glory of God; being justified freely by His grace through the redemption that is in Christ Jesus, whom God has set forth to be a propitiation through faith in His blood, to declare His righteousness for the remission of sins that are past.* **Rom. 3:22-25**

Q. Who are they that *hunger and thirst after righteousness*?

A. They who, while they love to do good, do not become proud, nor rest on their own good works, but admit that they are sinners and guilty before God; and who, through the prayer of faith, seek after justification of grace through Jesus Christ.

Q. What does the Lord promise to them who hunger and thirst after righteousness?

A. That they *shall be filled*.

Q. What is meant here by *filled?*

A. As the filling or satisfying of the body produces, first, an end to the sense of hunger and thirst, and second, the strengthening of the body by food; so the filling of the soul means, first, the inward peace of the pardoned sinner, and second, the ability to do good, given through justifying grace. The perfect filling, however, of the soul created for the enjoyment of eternal good, is to follow in the life eternal, according to the words of the Psalmist: *When I awake up after Thy likeness, I shall be satisfied with it.* **Ps. 17:15**

On the Fifth Beatitude:

Q. What is the Lord's fifth precept of blessedness?

A. They who would be blessed must be merciful.

Q. How are we to fulfill this precept?

A. By works of mercy, corporal and spiritual; for as St. John Chrysostom says, *the forms of mercy are manifold, and this commandment broad.* **Hom. on Mat. 15**

Q. Which are the corporal works of mercy?

A. 1. To feed the hungry.
2. To give drink to the thirsty.
3. To clothe the naked, or such as have not necessary and decent clothing.
4. To visit those who are in prison.
5. To visit the sick, minister to them, or aid them in Christian preparation for death.
6. To show hospitality to strangers.
7. To bury those who have died in poverty.

Q. Which are the spiritual works of mercy?

A. 1. By exhortation *to convert the sinner from the error of his way.* **James 5: 20**
2. To instruct the ignorant in truth and virtue.
3. To counsel our neighbor in times of difficulty.
4. To pray for others to God.
5. To comfort the afflicted.
6. Not to return the evil which others may have done to us.
7. To forgive injuries from our heart.

Q. Is it not contrary to the precept of mercy for civil justice to punish criminals?

A. Not in the least; if this be done as a duty, and with a good intent, that is, in order to correct them, or to preserve the innocent from their crimes.

Q. What does the Lord promise to the merciful?

A. That they *shall obtain mercy.*

Q. What specific kind of mercy is to be understood?

A. That of being delivered from everlasting condemnation for sin at God's Judgment.

On the Sixth Beatitude:

Q. What is the Lord's sixth precept for blessedness?

A. They who would be blessed must be *pure in heart.*

Q. Is not purity of heart the same thing as sincerity?

A. Sincerity which shows the really good disposition of the heart through good deeds is only the lowest degree of purity of heart. The greater form is attained by a constant and strict watchfulness over oneself, driving away from one's heart every unlawful wish and thought, and every attachment for earthly things, and ever preserving the remembrance of God and our Lord Jesus Christ with faith and charity.

Q. What does the Lord promise to the pure in heart?

A. That they *shall see God.*

Q. How are we to understand this promise?

A. The word of God compares the heart of man to the eye, and ascribed to perfect Christians *enlightened eyes of the heart.* **Ephes. 1:18** As the eye that is perceptive can see the light, so the heart that is pure can behold God. But since the sight of God's countenance is the very source of everlasting blessedness, the promise of seeing God is the promise of the highest degree of everlasting blessedness.

On the Seventh Beatitude:

Q. What is the Lord's seventh precept for blessedness?

A. They who would be blessed must be *peace-makers.*

Q. How are we to fulfill this commandment?

A. We must live peaceably with all men; if quarrels arise, we must try all possible ways to put a stop to it, even by yielding our own right, unless this be against duty, or hurtful to any other; if others are at odds, we must do all that we can to reconcile them, and if we fail, we must pray to God for their reconciliation.

Q. What does the Lord promise to the peace-makers?

A. That they *shall be called the Sons of God.*

Q. What is signified by this promise?

A. The sublimity both of their office and of their reward. Since in what they do they imitate the only-begotten Son of God, who came upon earth to reconcile fallen man with God's justice, they are for this act promised the gracious name of Sons of God, and without doubt a high degree of blessedness.

On the Eighth Beatitude:

Q. What is the Lord's eighth precept for blessedness?

A. They who would be blessed must be ready *to endure persecution for righteousness' sake,* without betraying it.

Q. What qualities are required by this precept?

A. Love of what is right, constancy and firmness in virtue, fortitude and patience when one is subjected to danger for refusing to betray truth and virtue.

Q. What does the Lord promise to those who are persecuted for righteousness' sake?

A. The *Kingdom of heaven.* In like manner the same is promised to the poor in spirit, to make up for the feeling of want and privation.

On the Ninth Beatitude:

Q. What is the Lord's ninth precept of blessedness?

A. They who would be blessed must be ready to take with joy reproach, persecution, suffering, and death itself, for the name of Christ, and for the true Christian faith.

Q. What is the name for the state required by this precept?

A. The state of Martyrdom.

Q. What does the Lord promise for this course?

A. *A great reward in heaven*; that is, a special and high degree of blessedness.

THE THIRD PART: ON CHARITY

On the Union between Faith and Charity:

Q. What should be the effect and fruit of true faith in the Christian?

A. Charity, or love, and good works. *In Jesus Christ,* says the Apostle Paul, *neither circumcision avails anything, nor uncircumcision, but faith which works by love.* **Gal. 5:6**

Q. Is not faith alone enough for a Christian, *without love and good works*?

A. No; for faith without love and good works is inactive and dead, and so cannot lead to eternal life. *He that loves not his brother, abides in death.* **I John 3:14**

What does it profit, my brethren, though a man say he has faith, and have not works? Can faith save him? For as the body without the spirit is dead, so faith without works is dead also. James 2:14,26

Q. May not a man on the other hand be saved by love and good works, without faith?

A. It is impossible that a man who has not faith in God should really love Him: besides, man, being ruined by sin, cannot do truly good works, unless he receives through faith in Jesus Christ spiritual strength, or grace from God. **Heb. 11:6; Gal. 3:10; Ib. 5:5; Ephes. 2:8,9**

Q. What is to be thought of love that is not accompanied by good works?

A. Such love is not real: for true love naturally shows itself by good works. Jesus Christ says: *He that has my commandments, and keeps them, he it is that love me; if a man love Me, he will keep My word.* **John 14:21,23**

The Apostle John writes: For this is the love of God, that we keep His commandments. **I John 5:3** Let us not love in word, neither in tongue, but in deed and in truth. **ib. 3:18**

On the Law of God and the Commandments:

Q. What means do we have to know good works form bad?

A. The inward law of God, or the witness of our conscience, and the outward law of God, or God's commandments.

Q. Does Holy Scripture speak of the inward law of God?

A. The Apostle Paul says of the heathen: *Which show the work of the law written in their hearts, their conscience also bearing witness, and their thoughts the meanwhile accusing or else excusing one another.* **Rom. 2:15**

Q. If there is in man's heart an inward law, why was the outward given?

A. It was given because men did not obey the inward law, but led carnal and sinful lives, and silenced within themselves the voice of the spiritual law, so that it was necessary to express this outwardly through the commandments. *Wherefore then serves the law? It was added because of transgressions.* **Gal. 3:19**

Q. When, and how, was God's outward law given to men?

A. When the Hebrew people, descended from Abraham, had been miraculously delivered from bondage in Egypt, on their way to the promised land, in the desert, on Mount Sinai, God manifested His presence in fire and clouds, and gave them the law, by the hand of Moses, their leader.

Q. Did Jesus Christ teach men to walk by the ten commandments?

A. He taught us that if we wished to attain everlasting life, to keep the commandments, and taught us to understand and fulfill them more perfectly, than had been done before He came. **Mat. 19:17, and 5**

On the Division of the Commandments into Two Tablets:

Q. What are the two divisions of the ten commandments?

A. Love of God, and love for our neighbor.

Q. Has not Jesus Christ taught the twofold commandments?

A. Jesus said: *Thou shalt love the Lord thy God with all thy heart, and with all thy soul, and with all thy mind. This is the first and greatest commandment. And the second is like unto it: "Thou shalt love thy neighbor as thyself." On these two commandments hang all the law and the prophets.* **Mat. 22:36-40**

Q. Are all men our neighbors?

A. Yes, all; because all are the creation of one God, and have come from one man: but our neighbors in faith are doubly neighbors to us, as being children of one heavenly Father by faith in Jesus Christ.

Q. But why is there no commandment of love to ourselves?

A. Because normally we love ourselves naturally, and without any commandment. *No man ever yet hated his own flesh, but nourishes it and cherishes it.* **Ephes. 5:29**

Q. What order should there be in our love of God, our neighbor, and ourselves?

A. We should love ourselves not for our own but for God's sake, and partly also for the sake of our neighbors: we should love our neighbor for the sake of God: but we should love God for Himself, and above all. Love of self should be sacrificed to the love of our neighbor; but both should be sacrificed to the love of God. *Greater love has no man than this, that a man lay down his life for his friends.* **John 15:13**

He that loves father or mother more than Me, said Jesus Christ, *is not worthy of Me: and he that loves son or daughter more than Me, is not worthy of Me.* **Mat. 10:37**

Q. If the whole law is contained in two commandments, why are they divided into ten?

A. In order to more clearly set forth our duties towards God, and towards our neighbor.

Q. What are the Ten Commandments?

A. 1. I am the Lord thy God; thou shalt not have strange gods before Me.
2. Thou shalt not take the name of the Lord thy God in vain.
3. Remember thou keep holy the Sabbath Day.
4. Honor thy father and thy mother.
5. Thou shalt not kill.
6. Thou shalt not commit adultery.
7. Thou shalt not steal.
8. Thou shalt not bear false witness against thy neighbor.
9. Thou shalt not covet thy neighbor's wife.
10. Thou shalt not covet thy neighbor's goods.

Q. Where do we find the Ten Commandments?

A. We find the Ten Commandments in the Book of Exodus, Chapter 20, verses 1-17.

Q. To whom did God give the Ten Commandments?

A. God gave the Ten Commandments to Moses, who in turn gave them to the Jewish people. **Ex. 31:18; Deut. 4:12-13; 5:22**

Q. Are we obliged to keep all the commandments?

A. Yes, we are obliged to keep the Ten Commandments, aided by the grace of God. **John 14:15,24; James 2:10; Deut. 5:32-33**

Q. What is the first commandment?

A. The first commandment is: *I am the Lord thy God; thou shalt not have strange gods before me.* **Ex. 20:1-3; Deut. 5:6-7**

Q. What does the first commandment require of us?

A. By the first commandment we are required to worship God as Creator of heaven and earth, and Him alone. **Luke 10:25-28; Deut. 6:4-5**

Q. What is forbidden by this commandment?

A. 1. To worship false gods;
2. To give to anything or anyone the worship due God alone.
3. To worship Him with false worship.
Lev. 26:1; Is. 42:8; John 4:22

Q. In what ways would this commandment be broken?

A. This commandment can be broken in the following ways:

1. Idolatry, the worship of images and false gods.
2. By attributing to persons or things power that belongs to God alone, *i.e.* fortune tellers, spiritualists, Ouija boards, and the like;
3. By the participation in heretical worship.

Q. How do we show our adoration to God?

A. We show our adoration to God by keeping His commandments, by praying to Him, and especially by our participation in the holy Sacrifice of the Mass. **John 4:24; Rom. 12:1-2; I Cor. 2:17-27**

Q. Do Old Catholics break the first commandment by having crucifixes, statues, icons, pictures, or relics in their churches?

A. No, for crucifixes, statues, icons, pictures, and relics simply represent the persons symbolized as an aid to prayer. **Num. 21:8; Ex. 20:5**

Q. What is the second commandment?

A. The second commandment is: *Thou shalt not take the name of the Lord thy God in vain.* **Ex. 20:7; Ez: 36:20-21; Rom. 2:24**

Q. When is God's name taken in vain?

A. God's Name is taken in vain whenever it is used improperly, especially when used in a lie or disrespectfully. **Lev. 5:4-5; II Chron. 32:16-17: Eccus. 23:9-12**

Q. What sins are forbidden by the second commandment?

A. The following sins are forbidden by the second commandment?
1. Blasphemy—daring words against God. **Ps 74:18**

2. Murmuring—complaining against God's Providence. **I Cor. 10:9-10**
3. Profanity—speaking lightly or irreverently about holy things. **Mal. 1:10-12**
4. Inattentiveness in prayer. **I Cor. 14:14-15**
5. Perjury—swearing a false oath. **Mat. 26:72**
6. Oath-breaking—breaking of promises. **Lev. 5:1,4**

Q. What is the third commandment?

A. The third commandment is; *Remember, thou keep holy the Sabbath Day.* **Ex. 20:8**

Q. Why did God command the Sabbath to be kept holy?

A. God commanded the Sabbath to be kept holy because on this day God rested from His work of Creation. **Ex. 20:2** Also, by Church law, we are to give equal reverence to the Holy Days of Obligation.

Q. Why do we keep holy the first day of the week instead of the Sabbath or seventh day?

A. We keep holy the first day of the week faithful to the example of the Apostles in the early Church, who held the Eucharist on the first day of the week in remembrance of the facts that Christ rose from the dead and the Holy Spirit descended on the Apostles on a Sunday. **John 20:1; Acts 2:1-13; Acts 20:7**

Q. How are Old Catholics obliged to keep Sunday holy?

A. Old Catholics are obliged to keep Sunday holy by:
1. Assisting at Mass on all Sundays;
2. Refraining from all unnecessary servile work. **Acts 20:7; Deut. 5:13,14**

Q. What would excuse one from the obligation of attending Sunday Mass?

A. The following reasons would excuse one from the obligation of attending Sunday Mass:
1. Illness;
2. Great distance from a church;
3. Necessary occupation;
4. A necessary act of Charity.

Q. What kinds of labor are permitted on Sunday?

A. Any absolutely necessary work is permitted on Sunday. **Mat. 12:1-13; Mark 3:4,5; Deut. 20:1**

Q. Besides attending Mass and abstaining from work, how are we recommended to spend Sundays?

A. We are encouraged to spend Sundays in a way befitting the Lord's Day. For example, attending services, spending time in prayer and spiritual reading, and wholesome relaxation with family and friends would be profitable ways of spending the Lord's Day.

Q. Are we permitted amusements on Sunday?

A. Yes, amusements and relaxation are permitted provided that they do not interfere with our religious obligations.

Q. What is the fourth commandment?

A. The fourth commandment is: *Honor thy father and thy mother.* **Deut. 5:16; Eph. 6:1,2; Mark 7:10**

Q. What does this commandment require of us?

A. This commandment requires that we:
1. Love and respect our parents, and obey them in all that is not sinful;
2. Respect and obey every lawful authority, both religious and civil;
Prov. 1:8; Eph. 6:1,2; Mark 7:10

Q. What is the fifth commandment?

A. The fifth commandment is: *Thou shalt not kill.* **Ex. 5:15; Rom. 13:9; Mat. 5:21**

Q. What is forbidden by this commandment?

A. The following are forbidden by this commandment:
1. The unjust taking of a human life, including that of the unborn, or one's own life.

2. Hatred, physical abuse, quarreling, or jealousy, because these may lead to killing or to the injury of ourselves or others. **I John 3:15; Mat. 5:21,22; Col. 3:8**

Q. What is the sixth commandment?

A. The sixth commandment is: *Thou shalt not commit adultery.* **Ex. 20: 4; I Cor. 6:18; Mat. 5:27**

Q. What is the sin of adultery?

A. Adultery is the act whereby married persons unlawfully give that love which they owe each other to someone else. Covered under this commandment is the obligation of the unmarried to remain chaste.

Q. What does the sixth commandment forbid?

A. The sixth commandment forbids, in addition to adultery, all impurity and immodesty in words, looks, and actions, whether alone or with others. **Gal. 5:19-21; Eph. 5:3,4; Mat. 5:28**

Q. What is the seventh commandment?

A. The seventh commandment is: *Thou shalt not steal.* **Deut. 5:19; Rom. 13:9; Jer. 22:13**

Q. What is forbidden by this commandment?

A. 1. It is forbidden to take anything that rightly belongs to someone else;
2. It is forbidden to destroy or injure the property or possessions of another person.
Lev. 19:15; Job 24:9; Ex. 23:8

Q. What does stealing include?

A. Stealing includes the following: robbery and burglary; graft and bribes; cheating and fraud; not paying bills, taxes, and debts; non-support of dependents; wasting time or materials on a job; and not paying a just wage to employees. **Lev. 19:11; Mat. 22:21; Luke 3:12-14**

Q. What in general are all people obliged to do by this commandment?

A. Everyone is obliged to respect and uphold the just rights of others. **Deut. 24:13-15; Tob. 4:15**

Q. If we have broken this commandment, what are we obliged to do?

A. We are obliged to give back anything that we have taken, and to repair any damage that we have caused, insofar, as it is possible to do so.

Q. If we have found some article of value, what are we obliged to do?

A. We are obliged to try to find the owner and return the article to him. **Lev. 5:4; Prov. 29:24; Eccus. 5:10**

Q. What is the eighth commandment?

A. The eighth commandment is: *Thou shalt not bear false witness against thy neighbor.* **Ex. 20:16; Deut. 5:20; Lev. 19:11**

Q. What is the meaning of this commandment?

A. By the eighth commandment we are commanded to speak the truth in all things, especially in what concerns the good name and honor of others. **Lev. 19:15; I Pet. 2:1; James 4:11**

Q. What is forbidden by this commandment?

A. The eighth commandment forbids lying, hurting someone's reputation, unjust criticism, gossip, insults, violating entrusted confidences, judging another's actions without evidence, publicizing the sins of another, and perjury. **Eph. 4:25; I Pet 3:10; James 1:26**

Q. Is it ever permissible to reveal the faults of another?

A. We are permitted to reveal the faults of another only to a person in authority, and only for the sake of fraternal correction and the avoidance of continued evil. **Gal. 6:1**

Q. What are we bound to do if we have injured the character of another unjustly?

A. We must do everything in our power to restore his good name by correcting the evil report we have spread against him. **Mat. 5:23-25**

Q. What is the ninth commandment?

A. The ninth commandment is: *Thou shalt not covet thy neighbor's wife.* **Ex. 20:17; Mat. 5:28; Deut. 5:21**

Q. What is forbidden by this commandment?

A. This commandment forbids all lustful thoughts or wishes, or inward adultery. **Mat. 5:28; Mark 7:21; James 1:14-15**

Q. Are involuntary, impure thoughts sinful?

A. No, but they become sinful when we knowingly and willingly entertain such thoughts.

Q. What is the tenth commandment?

A. The tenth commandment is *Thou shalt not covet thy neighbors goods.* **Ex. 27:28; Psalm 36:7; Eccus. 9:16**

Q. What is forbidden by the tenth commandment?

A. It is forbidden to envy the fortune of another, and to seriously lust after what belongs to another. **Luke 12:15**

A Treasury of Prayers

The Sign of the Cross

+ In the Name of the Father, and of the Son, and of the Holy Spirit. Amen.

A Morning Offering

O Jesus, through the prayers of the Mother of God, I offer Thee my prayers, works, joys and sufferings of this day for all the intentions of Thy Holy Will, in union with the Holy Sacrifice of the Mass throughout the World, in reparation for my sins, and for the intentions of all our associates.

The Lord's Prayer

Our Father, who art in heaven, hallowed be Thy name; Thy kingdom come; Thy will be done on earth as it is in heaven. Give us this day our daily bread; and forgive us our trespasses as we forgive those who trespass against us and lead us not into temptation but deliver us from evil. Amen.

The Hail Mary

Hail Mary, full of Grace the Lord is with thee. Blessed art thou among women and blessed is the fruit of thy womb Jesus. Holy Mary Mother of God, pray for us sinners now and at the hour of our death. Amen.

The Doxology

Glory be to the Father, and to the Son, and to the Holy Spirit. As it was in the beginning is now, and ever shall be world without end. Amen.

The Apostles' Creed

I believe in God, the Father Almighty, Creator of heaven and earth; And in Jesus Christ, His only Son, our Lord: Who was conceived by the Holy Spirit, born of the Virgin Mary, suffered under Pontius Pilate, was crucified, died, and was buried. He descended into hell; the third day He arose again from the dead, He ascended into heaven, and sits at the right hand of God, the Father Almighty; from thence He shall come to judge the living and the dead.

I believe in the Holy Spirit, the Holy Catholic Church, the Communion of Saints, the forgiveness of sins, the resurrection of the body, and the life of the world to come. Amen.

The Confiteor

I confess to almighty God, to blessed Mary ever a Virgin, to blessed Michael the archangel, to blessed John the Baptist, to the holy apostles Peter and Paul, to all the saints, that I have sinned exceedingly in thought, word, and deed, through my fault, through my fault, through my most grievous fault. Therefore I beg blessed Mary ever a Virgin, blessed Michael the archangel blessed John the Baptist, the Holy apostles Peter and Paul, and all the saints, to pray to the Lord our God for me.

May Almighty God have mercy on me, and having forgiven my sins, bring me to eternal life. Amen.

May the Almighty and merciful Lord grant me pardon, absolution, and remission of my sins. Amen.

A Short Act of Contrition

O my God! I am truly sorry for all my sins, because they have offended Thee, Who art all good and worthy of all my love. I firmly resolve by Thy holy grace never again to commit sin.

An Act of Faith

O my God! I firmly believe that Thou art one God in three Divine Persons, Father, Son, and Holy Spirit; I believe that Thy Divine Son became man, and died for our sins, and that He will come to judge the living and the dead. I believe these and all the truths which the Holy Catholic Church teaches, because Thou hast revealed them, Who canst neither deceive nor be deceived.

An Act of Hope

O my God! relying on Thy infinite goodness and promises, I hope to obtain pardon of my sins, the help of Thy grace, and life everlasting, through the merits of Jesus Christ, my Lord and Redeemer.

An Act of Love

O my God! I Love Thee above all things, with my whole heart and soul, because Thou art all-good and worthy of all love. I love my neighbor as myself for the love of Thee. I forgive all who have injured me, and ask pardon of all whom I have injured.

A Short Act of Contrtion

O my God! I give Thee thanks from the bottom of my heart, for the mercies and blessings which Thou hast bestowed upon me; above all because Thou hast loved me from all eternity, and hast sent Thy Divine Son, Our Lord Jesus Christ, to redeem me with His Precious Blood.

Blessings Before Meals

Bless, us O Lord, and these Thy gifts which we are about to receive from Thy bounty, through Christ our Lord. Amen.

O Christ our God, bless the food and drink of Thy servants, for Thou art Holy now and forever. Amen.

Blessings After Meals

We give Thee thanks for all Thy benefits, O Almighty God, who livest and reignest forever.

May the divine assistance remain always with us. And may the souls of the faithful departed, through the mercy of God, rest in peace. Amen.

A Prayer to my Guardian Angel

Angel of God, my guardian dear, to whom His love commits me here, ever this day be at my side, to light and guard, to rule and guide. Amen.

The Jesus Prayer

Lord Jesus Christ, Son of God, have mercy upon me a sinner.

The Seven Corporal Works of Mercy

1. To Feed the hungry.
2. To give drink to the thirsty.
3. To clothe the naked.
4. To visit the sick.
5. To harbor the harborless.
6. To visit and ransom the captives.
7. To bury the dead.

The Seven Spiritual Works of Mercy

1. To admonish the sinners.
2. To give instruction to the ignorant.

3. To give counsel to the doubtful.
4. To comfort those who sorrow.
5. To bear wrongs patiently.
6. To forgive all injuries.
7. To offer prayers for the living and the dead.

The Precepts of the Church

To keep holy Sundays and Holy Days.

To attend Mass on Sundays and Holy Days.

To observe the rules of fast and abstinence.

To confess our sins and receive Holy Communion at least once a year, during the Easter Time.

Not to solemnize marriage at forbidden times.

To pray daily—especially at the beginning and the end of the day.

To contribute to the support of the Church.

The Holy Days of Obligation

1. January 1—Circumcision
2. January 6—Epiphany
3. March 25—Annunciation
4. 40 Days after Easter—Ascension
5. August 6—Transfiguration
6. August 15—Assumption
7. November 1—All Saints
8. December 25—Christmas

The Three Theological Virtues

Faith, Hope, Charity.

The Four Cardinal Virtues

Prudence, Temperance, Justice, and Fortitude.

The Eucharistic Fast

All are encouraged to fast from midnight; however, a fast of three hours from solids (alcohol included) and one hour from liquids is sufficient. The sick and infirm need not fast at all.

Some Rules for Christian Living

Be diligent in your work and shun idleness.
Speak the truth at all times.
Know when to speak and when to remain silent.
Do not positively affirm or deny things you know nothing about.
Respect your elders—listen when they speak.
Be not proud or covetous.
Do not delay making amends to those you offend.
Be kind to others and they will be kind to you.
Observe neatness and cleanliness in your habits and dress.

An Examination of Conscience Before Confession

Before going to Confession the penitent should make a self-appraisal of personal shortcomings. For guidance, the following questions are suitable for self-examination of conscience:

Have you experienced doubts in your faith? Have you despaired of God's mercies and spoken against the Lord in time of adversity?

Have you attended church regularly? Have you prayed regularly, remembering other in your prayers? Have you kept the Sabbath holy and refrained from doing any unnecessary work on Sundays or Holy Days?

Have you observed Lent and kept the fasts of the Church? Have you attended dances or indulged in entertainments during Lent?

Have you put your belief into fortune tellers or consulted those who presume to predict the future?

Have you spoken lightly of religious matters or of sacred objects? Have you taken the name of God in vain? Have you cursed yourself or others?

Have you become angry at others or caused others to anger?

Have you honored your parents, superiors, teachers and spiritual advisors?

Have you shown respect to the infirm and the aged?

Have you oppressed anyone, held hatred for others, envied others or desired revenge on anyone? Have you injured anyone by word or deed? Have you caused strife between others? Have you desired or hastened the death of anyone?

Have you chosen your companions wisely? Have you willfully entertained impure thoughts or desires? Have you read obscene literature or been guilty of unchaste words or actions?

Have you taken any property belonging to others? Have you deceived anyone in business transactions? Have you coveted the possessions of others?

Have you witnessed falsely against anyone or passed unconfirmed judgment on anyone?

Have you partaken of confession and Holy Communion at least once a Year?

ENDNOTES FOR CHAPTER FIVE

[1.] The Old Catholic Church of America, *The Official Catechism of the Old Catholic Church of America*, Archbishop-Metropolitan James Bostwick. Used by permission, 2003.

6

Why Eastern and Western Expressions Combine In American Old Catholicism

Old Catholic Churches, not being a part of the Roman Catholic Communion, function in a non-hierarchical large-scale organization. As such is the case, the administration of Old Catholic parishes and dioceses are more collegial and less authoritarian in nature. While bishops maintain their traditional position as Elders and Shepherds of the local Church, determinations binding on the entire Church body are arrived at by the entire college of bishops and not mainly through one individual. Parish priests, while maintaining their traditional and scriptural role in the Church, empower the laity to be more operative in the missions and ministries of the Church, taking on roles as directing the efforts of the parish outreach programs, rather than relying on the pastor or assistant pastor to make the ministry successful.

The phenomenon of multiple Old Catholic jurisdictions within the Americas, required a method of establishing dialogue and inter-jurisdictional concordats drawn heavily on the model of relationships between the autocephalous Orthodox Churches of the East, which recognize the legitimacy of each other, and do not seek to usurp the existence of the other, but recognizes each as a sister Church in Christ. Since however, there exist organizations and churches possessing a theology that is markedly different from the faith described herein, strict examination to ensure a unity of theological belief was first required. Today there exists a confederacy of Old Catholic Churches in the Americas, with overlapping jurisdictions, which aid and support one another as members of one communion.

In addition, with the merging of faithful and of clergy, and as the result of working together towards common goals, American Old Catholics have been exposed to Eastern Orthodox theology and expressions of faith, through the early Russian Orthodox efforts in the Americas. In many cases Russian and Greek Orthodox origins of Apostolic Succession have found their way alongside the Old Catholic lines of Archbishop Mathew and the Oriental lines of Archbishop Vilatte, as autocephalous Orthodox bishops assisted in the consecrations of Old Catholic bishops in the Americas. Throughout the years, some Old Catholic Churches of American origin have been received into various Eastern Orthodox Churches. [1]

Like the Eastern Orthodox Churches, the Old Catholics respect the Roman Pontiff and accord to him the respect due also as "First among equals" as the Bishop of Rome. But also like the Eastern Orthodox, the Old Catholics reject the concept of the "universal jurisdiction" of the Pope over all of Christendom. Old Catholics affirm the Seven Oecumenical Councils of the entire Church, and the Nicene Creed without the *filioque*. Old Catholics adopted a polyvalent hermeneutical approach to understanding the foundational teachings of the Church so that, instead of Eastern or Western, in many cases, it is Eastern—and *also* Western expressions of Christian truth that are taught. It is this understanding of theology, before the Council of Trent, before Vatican Councils I & II that permeate Old Catholic teaching.

Like the Eastern Orthodox Churches, the Old Catholic understands that proper interpretation of Holy Scripture takes place in the community of the Church and not apart of it, nor as an individual. Consider the following:

"In order to 'read the Bible in the Church', one must recognize that the Spirit of God had indeed inspired Christians in the past to unfold the Scripture's meanings. By 'the past' I do not mean only those who lived in Reformation times, but those who studied the Scriptures for the previous fifteen centuries as well. These men are popularly called 'Fathers.' They are called Fathers because many of their interpretations have valiantly preserved and defended the messages of the Scriptures, often in the face of great persecution, and for this we respect them. If we want to be in touch with the Spirit's lessons to the *whole* Church, we cannot confine ourselves to the teachers of our own time.

Some of these Church Fathers were immediate disciples and successors of the Apostles. Clement (30-100), an early bishop of Rome, was an acquaintance of both Peter and Paul, and Ignatius of Antioch (30-107) and Polycarp of Smyrna (69-155) were disciples of the Apostle John. Noted Church historian Phillip Schaff recognizes these men, and others such as Papias (70-155), Barnabas (a letter of his dating 117/132), Hermas (140/155), and the unknown authors of the Epistle to Diogneus (150) and the Didache (100 AD-150), as 'The first church teachers after the apostles, who enjoyed in part personal [relationships]...with them...' Imagine the insight these men had! They learned from those who literally heard the very words of Christ with their own ears. Try to fathom the perspective they brought to the Scriptures! Is it really possible to consider ourselves serious students of the Scriptures if we choose to ignore what those earliest believers and martyrs had to say?" [2]

In addition, Eastern Orthodox, Roman Catholics and Old Catholics understand the Word of God to exist as more than merely words in print. The Word of God is also the living, breathing faith expressed by the believer, and it is revealed in communal membership with the Body of Christ, that is, His Church.

"God's Word is not bound by ink or held captive by bookbinding. His Word existed before the invention of books and would continue to exist even if every Bibles were destroyed. God's Word is the 'Living Voice' which those who have united themselves to Christ can bear witness to as being of God. Thus, God's Word is understood in *relationship*, not in reading. The early Church was in deep communion with God's Word not because they had a Bible, but *because they had a New Covenant relationship with the living Word, Jesus Christ.*

The Truth of God's Word has been revealed not only *to* God's People but *in* God's people (1 Cor. 2:9-13). This gives the members of the Church alone the ability to understand the Scripture *as* Scripture. This divinely orchestrated marriage of Spirit and humanity makes the Bible truly sufficient in the Church. Unlike the heretics, the Church's members recognize its true message, for the 'anointing of truth' which rests upon them lets them know the teaching (1 John 3:27). The Bible is *their* book and they are of 'like Spirit' with it. Their Christian life and experience, which includes the experiences of their brethren before them, attests to the Bible's true teaching." [3]

This expression naturally leads to this unanimous conclusion, agreed upon by all:

"Without question, the Scriptures are an invaluable and essential expression of Divine Tradition. But when they are set apart from the Holy Spirit's ministry in the Church, they are no longer 'a sure foundation.' Outside the Church, the Bible's stabilizing legs are cut off by contradictory interpretations of 'individuals.' Our call to understand the Scriptures in concert with the Church prevents such an abuse. But this attentiveness to the Church is no an exhortation to sleepily submit to an ecclesiastical court. It is a call to take responsibility; to evaluate the reasons behind our present beliefs instead of accepting them without question, to take the initiative to seek the mind of those who have gone before us, and to pursue personal interaction with their perspectives. Only then will we, in union with the brethren of all ages, be able to demonstrate the Bible Truth entrusted to us." [4]

ENDNOTES FOR CHAPTER SIX

[1] Karl Pruter, *A History of the Old Catholic Church,* (St. Willibrord's Press, 1973)

[2] Jordan Bajis, *Common Ground, An Introduction to Eastern Christianity For The American Christian,* Second Edition (Light and Life Publishing, 1989) p. 86-87.

[3] Ibid. p. 91.

[4] Ibid. p. 92.

7

Yesterday's Tomorrow, Today

The goals and expectations of the early Old Catholics in the Americas were not realized in their lifetime. We have seen, however, that their struggle has not been in vain, and the seed that was planted has grown. In spite of the many obstacles faced by early Old Catholics here in the Americas, some of their own doing, Old Catholics do today exist.

Living in the "information age" has breathed new life into Old Catholicism, allowing like-minded Old Catholic organizations to come together, pool their resources and establish Old Catholic parishes, missions and ministries. The Internet has allowed churches to communicate and let others know where they are and when they celebrate Mass. The Internet has, unfortunately, brought its own set of problems as well, giving a platform to a variety of individuals claiming tactile succession from the Old Catholic tradition, engaged in marginally Christian, and sometimes not Christian at all, types of activities. One must carefully scrutinize any church claiming to be "Old Catholic", to ensure that it does, in fact, conform to traditional, authentic and historic Old Catholic faith, practice and worship.

Churches are calling each other, clergy are talking and sharing ideas—and people are working together on a scale that has not been seen before. Old Catholic bodies of like theology are working together. An ongoing challenge for some parts of the greater Church movement, is to maintain the historic witness in an organization that is collegial and not rigidly hieratically authoritative. Some churches have given in to modernism, leaving the traditional faith of Old Catholicism to embrace innovations in the faith, and use a variety of identifiers, smoke and mirrors, to explain their non-Catholic beliefs. But one only has to look at the historic witness of the Faith of Old Catholics here in the Americas, and use it as a measuring stick, to determine whether what is proposed is genuine or not. Apostolic Tradition is giving the saints and martyrs of the Church a vote, the opportunity to guide us in what is and what is not Catholic.

Society's modern, anti-sacramental flavor has resulted in many people of strong faith to embrace the traditional, sacramental worship of Old Catholicism. Today's "culture of death" is programming society to accept euthanasia, abortion, the "right to die", and everyone is encouraged to be his or her own conscience and determiner of what is right and wrong, good or evil. God has, for many people, been relegated to the realms of things that don't really impact daily life...or for some, live at all. This consistent stripping away of hope, faith and a healthy spirituality has caused many people to wake up and seek out ancient Catholic Faith, Practice and Worship, and the Old Catholic Church in the Americas is growing, and growing fast.

The Old Catholic Church does not need to be a huge church, neither does it need to own large edifices and massive amounts of land, in order to be a viable, effective servant of God. The Old Catholic Church simply needs to faithfully witness the Good News of Christ, and tenaciously protect the Deposit of Faith entrusted to it. We are a city of refuge for those who wish to turn from sin, repent rejection of God's Word, and become an adopted son or daughter of God.

APPENDIX A

Treatise on the Married Episcopate

✦

AN ARGUMENT FROM TRADITION FOR ORDAINING MARRIED PRIESTS TO THE EPISCOPATE OF THE ORTHODOX CATHOLIC CHURCH

by Denis M. Garrison

Introduction

In the Orthodox Church in the New World, since early in the twentieth century, the concept of the married episcopate has been an important and urgent issue. The question has arisen with increasing frequency and force: Is it allowable to elect and consecrate married Priests to the episcopate and to allow them to persevere in the episcopate although they continue their married lives full and complete, co-habiting and maintaining their marital relations with their wives? Since the 6th Ecumenical Council, the discipline of Holy Church has been to prohibit the married episcopate, while still strongly maintaining the married diaconate and presbyterate. This discipline has been adhered to since with varying degrees of fidelity in various parts of the world, but it is fair to characterize this discipline as generally uniform throughout Holy Church.

This question came to be of particular importance after His Eminence, Archbishop Aftimios Ofiesh of blessed memory, married Miss Mariam Namey in 1933, many years after he was consecrated to the episcopate. Abp. Aftimios acted out of conviction that the married episcopate is truly Scriptural; furthermore, he was reacting to great scandals in the Orthodox Church involving the celibate clergy (such scandals are still common today). Abp. Aftimios also was moved to marry by his desire to force the issue of the married episcopate to consideration by a Pan-Orthodox Council; a wish which was thwarted then, but may yet be fulfilled. While Abp. Aftimios thereupon retired from the hierarchy of the Church, the remaining Bishops of his jurisdiction made it clear that they thought his expressed belief that the episcopate should include married men was correct and scripturally sound. Since that time, a number of Bishops succeeding after Abp. Aftimios, including several Primates, have been elected from the married presbyterate and have remained married as Bishops. This discipline, election of married Priests to the episcopate without requiring them to separate from their wives, is also followed in a number of the smaller Orthodox jurisdictions in the Americas; but the earlier discipline, prohibition of the married episcopate, is still maintained in the "main-line Orthodox Churches," as well as by traditionalist ethnic jurisdictions. It is accurate, therefore, to say that the issue of the married episcopate is controversial within Holy Church in this time and place.

I, myself, am a Bishop and a husband; I was married several years before I was ordained. I was consecrated Bishop in 1985. Since my consecration I have maintained my marital life unamended and hope to do so throughout my life. I believe that the Sacrament of Holy Orders, at any rank, cannot and must not vitiate the Sacrament of Holy Matrimony. I mention this so that the reader knows my analysis of the issues herein is inescapably tempered by my own marital and clerical status. Nevertheless, I believe my analysis to be objectively fair and accurate, or else I would not dare to publish it.

Marriage Before Ordination

"No Bishop, Presbyter, or Deacon shall put away his own wife under pretext of reverence. If, however, he put her away, let him be excommunicated; and if he persist in so doing, let him be deposed from office."—[Canon V of the Holy Apostles]

In accordance with the most ancient tradition, the consolation of the Holy Sacrament of Matrimony should not be denied to men who wish to receive the Sacrament of Holy Orders at a later date. It seems obvious that, just as a man, whether single or married to an Orthodox woman, may be tonsured and ordained as a Church Servitor, or a Subdeacon, or a Deacon, or a Priest, if he is otherwise qualified, likewise, a Priest, single or married to an Orthodox woman, should be allowed to be consecrated to the sacred episcopate, if he is otherwise qualified, in accordance with Canon V of the Holy Apostles. Membership in the episcopate ought not to be restricted to monks. In this time of great scarcity of monks, the married clergy necessarily are a resource from which the episcopate must be drawn.

"Whoever has entered into two marriages after baptism, or has possessed himself of a concubine, cannot be a Bishop, or a Presbyter, or a Deacon, or anything else in the Sacerdotal List."—[Canon XVII of the 85 Canons of the Holy Apostles]

"No one who has taken a widow, or a divorced woman, or a harlot, or a house maid, or any actress as his wife, may be a Bishop, or a Presbyter, or a Deacon, or hold any other position at all in the Sacerdotal List."—[Canon XVIII of the 85 Canons of the Holy Apostles]

A man who has married a second time cannot be ordained a Subdeacon, a Deacon, a Priest, or a Bishop, according to Canon XVII of the 85 Canons of the Holy Apostles. *"Whoever has entered into two marriages after baptism"* (Canon XVII) reflects the fact that, under the very strictest understanding, for a man to marry twice is adultery of a sort on his part. The rules about *"a widow, or a divorced woman"* (Canon XVIII) do not disparage those women's morality; rather, they were already married once, and therefore, again under the strictest understanding, to marry such a woman is adultery of a sort. (See Matthew 5:32 and 19:7-9.) While second (and even third) marriages may be allowed, for the weakness of the flesh, to the laity, the clergy are called to be irreproachable and, therefore, the clergy are not allowed to marry widows or divorced women.

We rarely use the word *"concubine"* (Canon XVII) in these days; we interpret *"concubine"* to refer to any woman with whom the man has entered into any kind of illicit sexual relationship. Also, in this modern age, we interpret *"a harlot, or a house maid, or any actress"* (Canon XVIII) to refer to any woman of infamous reputation or who is known for her moral turpitude. The occupations of domestic servants and actresses in the modern world cannot honestly be generically maligned as immoral; rather, it is marriage with any woman who is in any occupation which can honestly be characterized as immoral (for example, prostitution) which is prohibited. As Canons XVII and XVIII both plainly imply, a man who has married within these Canons and who is otherwise qualified may indeed be ordained *"a Bishop, Presbyter, or Deacon, or anything else in the Sacerdotal List."*

Marriage After Ordination

"As to bachelors who have entered the clergy, we allow only anagnosts (Readers) and psalts (Chanters) to marry, if they wish to do so."—*[Canon XXVI of the 85 Canons of the Holy Apostles] (See also Canon XIV of the 4th Ecumenical Council and Canon VI of the 6th Ecumenical Council.)*

Also in accordance with ancient tradition, the sacred clergy in Holy Orders should not feel free to marry at will. The Church may exercise discipline in this matter, as seems prudent and expedient at the time and place. A Church Servitor who was a bachelor when he was ordained has the right to marry an Orthodox woman, in accordance with Canon XXVI of the Holy Apostles and Canon XIV of the 4th Ecumenical Council (451 A.D.). A Subdeacon, Deacon, Priest, or Bishop who is a bachelor, once he is ordained, is not permitted marriage thereafter by Canon XXVI. Yet, traditionally, we may make exceptions: a Subdeacon or Deacon who announced before his ordination to his ordaining Bishop that he plans to marry may be dispensed from this prohibition, by the same Bishop or his successor, to marry after ordination, in accordance with Canon X of Ancyra. Thus, the principle of allowing, by the exercise of Economy, ordained clergy to marry and remain clergy is well established in ancient precedent. We respect the ancient tradition which discourages men already in holy orders from marrying and encourages special caution regarding the marriages of ordained clergy. However, in light of the permissive precedents established by Canon XXVI of the Holy Apostles, Canon XIV of the 4th Ecumenical Council, and Canon X of Ancyra, and considering a footnote to Canon V of the Holy Apostles which states that *"the custom prevailed of not letting those in holy orders marry…"*, showing that this was a custom rather than a necessary discipline, we cannot absolutely condemn marriage after ordination.

It seems to us that when Abp. Aftimios married, this very provocative act catalyzed the active reconsideration in Holy Church of this issue of the married episcopate. Prior to his marriage, the occasional married Bishop (there were some) was not publicly approved by the Church, but was tolerated and kept quiet. Once the issue was publicly raised, the discovery of the scriptural truth and the reaffirmation of the Apostolic teaching in this regard became more possible.

The continuing existence of Le Sacre Orientale Chiesa di Gesu Cristo Italo-Greca Ortodosso (the Holy Eastern Orthodox Italo-Greek Church of Jesus Christ), with its married episcopate and centuries of Orthodox witness, and the existence in the United States of its Italo-Greek Orthodox Christian Archdiocese, along with the witness of several small Orthodox jurisdictions with married Bishops, give us hope that the facade of ecumenical unanimity amongst Orthodox Churches on banning the married episcopate will one day fall away and the anomalous and anti-evangelical practice of an exclusively-monastic episcopate will be finally overthrown in Holy Church.

The Primary Issue: Married Bishops

Some of our brethren in the Eastern Churches may object to allowing married men to be consecrated as Bishops, for the discipline generally current throughout Orthodoxy at this time is that only monks may be consecrated as Bishops. It behooves us, therefore, to examine the matter of the married episcopate in the light of Holy Scripture and the Sacred Canons of the Church.

Holy Scripture—The Holy Apostle Paul gave explicit and clear directions in his epistles: *"A bishop then must be blameless, the husband of one wife…"*—(I Timothy 3:2); and again, *"ordain elders in every city…. If any be blameless, the husband of one wife,…for a Bishop must be blameless…."* (Titus 1:5-7). (The word *"blameless"* is best translated as *"irreproachable,"* according to <u>The Rudder (Pedalion)</u>. The Orthodox Church agrees, as attested by St John Chrysostom (noted in the Interpretation of Canon XII of the 6th Ecumenical Council), that the word *"elders"* in the original means *"bishops."*) But how should Bishops deal with their wives? *"Art thou bound unto a wife? Seek not to be loosed."*—(I Corinthians 7:27) *"Defraud (deprive) ye not one the other, except it be with consent for a time, that ye may give yourselves to fasting and prayer; and come together again, that Satan tempt you not for your incontinency."*—(I Corinthians 7:5) *"Marriage is honorable in all, and the bed undefiled:…"*—(Hebrews 13:4); for a Bishop to shun his wife would make it apparent that he dishonors marriage, and that he thinks bed and intercourse to be impure, but the Apostle calls marriage *"honorable"* and bed and intercourse *"undefiled."* During His Sermon on the Mount, the Lord said, *"But I say unto you, That whosoever shall put away his wife, saving for the cause of fornication, causeth her to commit adultery; and whosoever shall marry her that is divorced committeth adultery."*—(Matthew 5:32; see also Matthew 19:7-9). The Lord also said, *"What therefore God hath joined together, let not man put asunder."*—(Matthew 19:6). By the clear testimony of Holy Scripture, a man who is married to one woman may be a Bishop, and he is in most grave error if he shuns her bed or divorces her for any reason other than fornication.

Therefore, only a hypocrite could argue that Holy Scripture forbids the married episcopate. Indeed, the manner in which the Apostle Paul writes in his epistles, I Timothy (3:2) and Titus (1:5-7), suggests that the married episcopate was even normative. Further, the other Scriptures cited above make it unmistakably clear that any married man, including a Bishop, must respect and honor his marriage, including intimate relations with his wife, and that it is grave error to divorce his wife or to entirely shun intimate relations with her. It is impossible to enforce, as having doctrinal significance, any Canon which actually contradicts the clear meaning of the Holy Scriptures. Hence, the Canons to which we subscribe are those which are most truly consistent with the Holy Scriptures.

The Sacred Canons—*The 85 Canons of the Holy and Renowned Apostles* is the first collection of Sacred Canons in the authoritative and official English-language text of the Sacred Canons, The Rudder (Pedalion). These Canons are those which are considered by many to have been promulgated by the Holy Apostles themselves (either by all of them together or perhaps only by Saint Paul and Saint Peter) through Clement, the Bishop of Rome. (*See pages lvii through lxi of The Rudder (Pedalion) for a discussion of the apostolic origin of these Canons.*) These Canons are of the highest degree of importance to us, being apostolic in origin.

First and most importantly, Canon V of the 85 Canons of the Holy Apostles, which I cited earlier, makes it explicit and clear beyond any honest argument that the ancient tradition of the Holy Church recognized, valued, and positively promoted the married episcopate.

"No Bishop, Presbyter, or Deacon shall put away his own wife under pretext of reverence. If, however, he put her away, let him be excommunicated; and if he persist in so doing, let him be deposed from office."—*(Canon V of the Holy Apostles).*

This Canon reflects the equally explicit and clear directions of the Holy Apostle Paul to Timothy and Titus. Only a hypocrite could argue that Canon V of the Holy Apostles can be interpreted, in any manner whatsoever, to forbid the episcopate to married men. A footnote to Canon V of the Holy Apostles in The Rudder (Pedalion) explicitly states: *"Please note that in old times it was permissible for bishops to have wives."* The footnote gives the following as cases in point: *"Felix, the bishop of Rome, was a son of a priest named Felix, Pope Agapetus was a son of a presbyter named Gordianus. Pope Gelasius was a son of a bishop named Valerius, and many others were sons of priests."* The footnote goes on to state that it was Canon

XII of the 6th Ecumenical Council which sanctioned the custom of the married clergy except that *"bishops alone should not be allowed to have wives."*

Those who now forbid the episcopate to married men (viz., most Eastern Orthodox jurisdictions) cite other Canons as the bases for their discipline in this matter. Therefore, we must ask ourselves if Canon V of the 85 Canons of the Holy Apostles was ever rejected by the Ecumenical Councils and rendered ineffective. The answer is quite inescapable: both Canon II of the 6th Ecumenical Council and Canon I of the 7th Ecumenical Council explicitly accept and ratify all of the 85 Canons of the Holy Apostles. Moreover, Canon XIII of the 6th Ecumenical Council verifies verbatim Canon V of the 85 Canons of the Holy Apostles, but unjustifiably excepts Bishops from its applicability. Canon V of the Holy Apostles always was and still is a Sacred Canon of Holy Church.

"Whoever has entered into two marriages after baptism, or has possessed himself of a concubine, cannot be a Bishop, or a Presbyter, or a Deacon, or anything else in the Sacerdotal List."—(Canon XVII of the 85 Canons of the Holy Apostles)

"No one who has taken a widow, or a divorced woman, or a harlot, or a house maid, or any actress as his wife, may be a Bishop, or a Presbyter, or a Deacon, or hold any other position at all in the Sacerdotal List."—(Canon XVIII of the 85 Canons of the Holy Apostles)

These two Canons, XVII and XVIII, also cited earlier, both plainly imply that a man who has married acceptably can be *"a Bishop, or a Presbyter, or a Deacon, or anything else in the Sacerdotal List;"* otherwise, the prohibitions contained in the Canons would be moot and absurd with regard to Bishops.

Canon XL of the 85 Canons of the Holy Apostles directs that the difference between the property of the Bishop and the property of the Church be publicly known, and it prohibits a Bishop both from leaving the property of the Church to his wife and family and from depriving his wife and family from their rightful inheritance by leaving his own property to the Church through there being confusion as to whose the property really is. This Canon plainly takes for granted that some Bishops will have wives, whose inheritance could be at issue.

"If any Bishop, or Presbyter, or Deacon, or anyone at all on the sacerdotal list, abstains from marriage, or meat, or wine, not as a matter of mortification, but out of an abhorrence thereof, forgetting that all things are exceedingly good, and that God made man male and female, and blasphemously misrepresenting God's work of cre-

ation, either let him mend his ways or let him be deposed from office and expelled from the Church. Let a layman be treated similarly."—[Canon LI of the Holy Apostles]

This Canon LI plainly assumes that there will be men who do not abstain from marriage who will be Bishops, Presbyters, and Deacons. It is those **who have refused** to marry who are at risk of deposition from the clerical state and expulsion from Holy Church under this Canon. This Canon is an eloquent witness to the high regard that the Apostolic Church had for marriage, and explicitly for the marriage of Bishops, Presbyters, and Deacons. It witnesses to the Orthodox and unchangeable truth of the Christian Faith that *"all things are exceedingly good,"* and that it is blasphemous to misrepresent God's work of creation by holding that certain things (including lawful sexual relations, meat, and wine, which are simply those things about which errors arose early on) are in themselves unclean, and that it is blasphemous to abhor them.

What then are the true and allowable sacrifices? *"The sacrifices of God are a broken spirit: a broken and a contrite heart, O God, Thou wilt not despise."*—Psalm 51, Verse 17.

Further, the Apostle Paul calls marriage honorable and marital relations undefiled: *"Marriage is honorable in all, and the bed undefiled:...."*—[Hebrews 13:4]; and our Lord Jesus Christ sanctified marriage by His attendance at the marriage feast in Cana; thus it is un-Christian and anti-scriptural to consider bed and intercourse to be impure. Yet, despite the Orthodox Faith, and despite Canon LI of the Holy Apostles, beginning with the Council of Carthage and culminating in the 6th Ecumenical Council, the hierarchs of the Church enacted Canons which suppressed the marital relations and even the marriages of the clergy. The 6th Ecumenical Council could have condemned those in Africa who wished to suppress the marriages of the clergy, as they did with the very same situation in Rome, but they did not. Instead, they unreasonably and unjustifiably extended a ban on married Bishops throughout the world; this was obviously the result of the erroneous anti-marital sentiment which had become generally accepted since marital relations had come to be viewed, blasphemously, as unclean, particularly for a minister of the Sacraments.

The Heresy of Neo-Manichaeism

The term "Neo-Manichaeism" is more accurate and precise than the term "Puritanism," which was used in the prior edition of this Treatise.

"Neo-Manichaeism," as used herein, refers to the heretical impulse behind various erroneous doctrines which call for a more austere and rigid physical purity than is proper and correct according to the teaching of Christ our Lord and His faithful Apostles and disciples. The concept of impurity and purity as being susceptible of physical expression predated Christianity by many centuries; it appeared again in the heresies of the Manichees, Gnostics, and others.

Neo-Manichaeism refers specifically to heretical doctrines within Orthodox Catholicism which mirror the particular heresy of the Manichees, who combined Zoroastrianism, Gnostic Christianity, and pagan elements. Zoroastrianism, the pre-Islamic Persian religion, included a belief in an afterlife and in the continuous struggle of the universal spirit of good (Ormazd) with the spirit of evil (Ahriman), the good ultimately to prevail. Gnostic Christianity included this theological dualism and therefore despised the body as being evil and considered the soul to be trapped within the body.

The Manichees' fundamental dualistic theological concepts, of a spirit of good and a spirit of evil, on an essentially equal footing, that is, of two contending principles of good (light, God, the soul) and evil (darkness, Satan, the body), are antithetical to Orthodox Christianity which holds the fundamental monotheistic belief in One God, Who is all-good and all-powerful, and Who is opposed by Satan and the other fallen angels (i.e., the demons), all of whom are inferior to God in every respect. Canon LI of the Holy Apostles, cited above, confirms the Orthodox Faith: *"that all things are exceedingly good, and that God made man male and female"* and that abhorrence of marriage is a *"blasphemous misrepresentation of God's work of creation."*

The anti-Christian dualism of such *Neo-Manichaeism* demands compliance with laws of external cleanliness of the sort denounced by Jesus in the 23rd Chapter of Matthew. Jesus Christ taught us that it is not external things, but what comes from his heart that makes a man clean or unclean.

"And he called the multitude, and said unto them, 'Hear and understand: Not that which goeth into the mouth defileth a man; but that which cometh out of the mouth; this defileth a man.'" And after His disciples reported that the Pharisees were offended

by this saying, Jesus said: "Do not ye yet understand, that whatsoever entereth in at the mouth goeth into the belly, and is cast out into the draught? But those things which proceed out of the mouth come forth from the heart; and they defile the man. For out of the heart proceed evil thoughts, murders, adulteries, fornications, thefts, false witness, blasphemies. These are the things which defile a man; but to eat with unwashen hands defileth not a man."—[Matthew 15:11 and Matthew 15:17-20]

This divine instruction is a hard saying for many people; it is particularly hard for a few of those who have put their feet on the path of monasticism. It seems that there are some monastics who do not know, or cannot keep in mind, that they abstain from some things (e.g., marriage, meat, wine) because they wish to mortify the flesh and grow spiritually stronger (this is truly Orthodox, to sacrificially abstain from good things). Too many believe that they abstain from things which are unclean, thus making themselves more pure for God (this is the heresy of *Neo-Manichaeism*). Such an attitude leads to erroneous anti-marital policies. This is **not** Apostolic Christianity; this is the error of men. Witness the Orthodox, Apostolic Canon LI.

Neo-Manichaeism, which Canon LI reveals to be outright blasphemy, and the hypocrisy which promotes and defends it, seem to be the abiding sins of the institutional Churches, East and West, because men seek ritual purity on the basis of their own wisdom, despite the fact that God, in His wisdom, redeemed the whole world and all things are good in His eyes. *Neo-Manichaeism* is the result of the rejection of this very important and fundamental teaching of Christ. **Neo-Manichaeism is heresy!** When those who are perhaps most prone to falling into the error of *Neo-Manichaeism* are also the sole hierarchs of the Church (that is, with the exclusively-monastic episcopate which has been imposed upon Holy Church since the 6th Ecumenical Council), the danger of further distorting the Christian Faith in favor of *Neo-Manichaeism* obviously is very much increased. Of course, since virtually all Bishops have been monks for over a thousand years, the reversal of this erroneous trend will occur only by a great movement of the Holy Spirit. How, then, did a Canon forbidding the married episcopate come to be? Canon XII of the 6th Ecumenical Council is the primary basis for the currently widespread discipline of forbidding the married episcopate.

"And this too has come to our knowledge, that both in Africa and Libya and other regions the most God-beloved Presidents (Bishops) there continue living with their own wives even after the ordination has been conferred upon them, and will not abandon their wives, thus becoming an object of offense and a scandal to others. We

have therefore made it a matter of great concern to us to do everything possible for the benefit of the flocks under hand, and it has seemed best not to allow such a thing to occur hereafter at all. We assert this, however, not with any intention of setting aside or overthrowing any legislation laid down Apostolically, but having due regard for the salvation and safety of peoples and for their better advancement with a view to avoiding any likelihood of giving anyone cause to blame the priestly polity. For the divine Apostle says: 'Do all everything for the glory of God. Give none offense, neither to the Jews, nor to the Greeks, nor to the Church of God; even as I try to please all men in everything, without seeking any advantage of mine own, but the advantage of the many in order that they may be saved. Become ye imitators of me, just as I also am (an imitator) of Christ.' [I Corinthians 10:32-33 and 11:1]. If anyone should be shown to be doing this, let him be deposed from office."—[Canon XII of the 6th Ecumenical Council]

Canon XIII of the 6th Ecumenical Council deals with the then current Roman discipline which required ordinands to the Diaconate and Presbyterate to *"solemnly promise to have no further intercourse with their wives."* Canon XIII cites the long tradition (discussed above) of the married clergy and decrees that the Roman discipline is an error.

"Since we have learned that in the church of the Romans it is regarded as tantamount to a canon that ordinands to the deaconry or presbytery must solemnly promise to have no further intercourse with their wives. Continuing, however, in conformity with the ancient canon of apostolic rigorism and orderliness, we desire that henceforward the lawful marriage ties of sacred men become stronger, and we are nowise dissolving their intercourse with their wives, nor depriving them of their mutual relationship and companionship when properly maintained in due season, so that if anyone is found to be worthy to be ordained a Subdeacon, or a Deacon, or a Presbyter, let him nowise be prevented from being elevated to such a rank while cohabiting with a lawful wife. Nor must he be required at the time of ordination to refrain from lawful intercourse with his own wife, lest we be forced to be downright scornful of marriage, which was instituted by God and blessed by his presence, as attested by the unequivocal declaration of the Gospel utterance: 'What therefore God hath joined together, let no man put asunder' [Matthew 19:6]; and the Apostle's teaching: 'Marriage is honorable in all, and the bed undefiled' [Hebrews 13:4]; and 'Art thou bound unto a wife? seek not to be loosed.' [I Corinthians 7:27]. We are cognizant, though, that those who met in Carthage and made provision of decency in the life of ministers declared that Subdeacons and Deacons and Presbyters, busying themselves as they do with the sacred mysteries, according to their rules are obliged to practice temperance in connection with

their helpmates, in order that we may likewise keep the injunction handed down through the Apostles, and continued from ancient times in force, well knowing that there is a proper season for everything, and especially for fasting and prayer. For those who assist in the ceremonies of the sacrificial altar have to be temperate in all things at the time when they are handling holy things, so that they may be able to gain whatever they ask God for. If, therefore, anyone acting contrary to the Apostolic Canons require any person who is in sacred orders—any Presbyter, we mean, or Deacon, or Subdeacon—to abstain from intercourse and association with his lawful wife, let him be deposed from office. Likewise, if any Presbyter or Deacon expel his own wife on the pretext of reverence, let him be excommunicated; and if he persist, let him be deposed from office."—[Canon XIII of the 6th Ecumenical Council]

The omission of *"Bishop"* from the list of persons in sacred orders in Canon XIII of the 6th Ecumenical Council is very significant, reflecting Canon XII, which deprived Bishops of the rights of marriage. Thus, Canon XII commits wholesale the very offense (violation of Canon V of the Holy Apostles) for which, in the individual cases of Priests, Deacons, and Subdeacons, Canon XIII excommunicates and deposes!

In Canon XII, the 6th Ecumenical Council legislates in direct contradiction to Canon V of the Holy Apostles (while self-consciously declaring *"We assert this, however, not with any intention of setting aside or overthrowing any legislation laid down Apostolically...."*), and in direct contradiction of the Holy Scriptures [Matthew 5:32 and 19:6-9; I Corinthians 7:5 and 7:27; Hebrews 13:4; I Timothy 3:2; and Titus 1:5-7]; and then, immediately in Canon XIII, the 6th Ecumenical Council legislates precisely on the basis of Canon V of the Holy Apostles and Holy Scriptures (*"If, therefore, anyone acting contrary to the Apostolic Canons require any person who is in sacred orders.... Likewise, if any Presbyter or Deacon expel his own wife on the pretext of reverence,...."*) The kindest characterization which one might make is that Canon XII is anomalous and wholly inconsistent with the entire meaning and import of Canon XIII. One could, therefore, paraphrase Canons XII and XIII to implicitly say: *"If, therefore, anyone acting contrary to the Apostolic Canons require any person who is in sacred orders—any Bishop, we mean—to abstain from intercourse and association with his lawful wife, **let him be**. Likewise, if any Bishop expel his own wife on the pretext of reverence, **let him be**."*

Isn't that absurd? This is in direct contradiction to the Apostolic Canons and to the very arguments used by the same Council for Canon XIII! Remember, *"No Bishop, Presbyter, or Deacon shall put away his own wife under pretext of reverence.*

If, however, he put her away, let him be excommunicated; and if he persist in so doing, let him be deposed from office."—[Canon V of the Holy Apostles.]

Thus, Canon XII of the 6th Ecumenical Council is an **anti-evangelical** and (vis-a-vis Canon V and Canon LI of the Holy Apostles) an **anti-canonical** attack on the marriages of Bishops.

There were two primary causes for this anomalous and illegitimate legislation.

First and most disturbing, there was a longstanding and accelerating trend of excessive disparagement of marriage (this has disturbing undercurrents of the widely held pre-Christian concept of ritual purity; remember that the Apostle Paul calls marriage honorable and marital relations undefiled: *"Marriage is honorable in all, and the bed undefiled:...."*—[Hebrews 13:4]; thus it is anti-scriptural to consider marital relations to be impure) and also of excessive exaltation of monasticism. Monastic excesses have proven to be a bitter fruit of the heresy of *neo-Manichaeism*. This was the unspoken subtext of Canon XII, and of other later Canons which suppressed the marital relations and even the marriages of the clergy. Excessive exaltation of monasticism and disparagement of marriage is an anti-evangelical error which still besets the Orthodox Churches. It is not at all overstating the case to frankly define *misagomy* (hatred of marriage) and *misogyny* (hatred of women) as both being blasphemous (as is proven by Canon LI of the Holy Apostles) and heretical (being premised on the *neo-Manichaen* tenet that the body is evil and impure). [Obviously, *misandry* (hatred of males), as held by some modern radical feminists and others, is identically blasphemous and heretical.]

The second cause for the anomalous legislation of Canon XII was the proximate cause: the scandal caused the faithful in North Africa by their married Bishops. This may have been a good reason to ban married Bishops in North Africa, but not throughout the world. Yet, this concession to the priests in Barbary, Africa was not given to the Roman clergy (see Canon XIII of the 6th Ecumenical Council) because the Romans were considered more docile regarding morals, while the African were considered to have a wild character.

The interpretation of Canon XXX of the 6th Ecumenical Council (*see below*) notes that the Africans had *"a strange notion of what constitutes good order as respecting ecclesiastical morals, according to Balsamon, and [a] lack of firmness of faith....* "Thus, the Council could have as well condemned those who were scandalized in Africa, as they did in Rome, but they chose not to.

The unreasonable and unjustifiable extension of the ban on married Bishops throughout the world obviously was the result of the Council's hidden agenda, viz., the erroneous anti-marital sentiment discussed above. Let us look beyond Canons XII and XIII of the 6th Ecumenical Council, at additional canonical evidence of this error.

"Wishing to do everything for the edification of the Church, we have decided to make concessions to priests in Barbarian churches, so that if they are seeking to circumvent Apostolic Canon V by not expelling their wife, on the pretext of reverence, and to do what is beyond the limits set by it, by coming to a private agreement with their spouses to abstain from intercourse with each other. We decree that these priests shall cohabit with their wives no more, in any manner whatsoever, so as to afford us thereby positive proof that they are carrying out their promise. We make this concession to them, not for any other reason, but because of the pusillanimity of their thought, and the bizarre character of their ideas of morality, and the unsettled state of their mind."—[Canon XXX of the 6th Ecumenical Council]

Canon XXX discards the unnatural crypto-celibacy within cohabitation legislated in Canon XXXIII of Carthage (*see below*). Also, this Canon is quite clear that the Barbarian discipline was a circumvention of Canon V of the Holy Apostles. Nonetheless, the Council distorted the Tradition by allowing marriage to be dishonored amongst the Barbarians, against the clear teaching of the Holy Scriptures (not to mention Canon IV of Gangra (*see below*) and Canons V and LI of the Holy Apostles) because the Barbarians were pusillanimous and bizarre.

If the Ecumenical Council could so distort the Tradition by allowing marriage to be dishonored on the basis of applying Economy for pusillanimous and bizarre people, perhaps the Orthodox Churches of today, by Economy, might permit **us** to **honor** marriage, even amongst Bishops, in conformity with the clear teaching of Holy Scriptures and the ancient Canons.

Canon XII and Canon XXX of the 6th Ecumenical Council, and Canons III, IV, and XXXIII of Carthage (*see below*) all embody a conscious policy of appeasement of those who are demonstrably and admittedly in error. Appeasement is always and everywhere a bad policy since it seeks to mollify evil (thus belying truth) rather than to confront and overcome evil. This appeasement is hidden under a cloak of not wanting to give offense: *"We assert this, however, not with any intention of setting aside or overthrowing any legislation laid down Apostolically, but having due regard for the salvation and safety of peoples and for their better advancement with a view to avoiding any likelihood of giving anyone cause to blame the priestly polity. For the divine Apostle says: 'Do all everything for the glory of God. Give none offense,'"*—[Canon XII of the 6th Ecumenical Council]. Certainly, the self-same 6th Ecumenical Council did not stop at offending the Romans by name in Canon XIII. But the real impetus, of course, was the hidden agenda—the growing heresy of *neo-Manichaeism*, pursuing *"ritual purity."*

"If anyone discriminates against a married Presbyter, on the ground that he ought not to partake of the offering when that Presbyter is conducting the Liturgy, let him be anathema."—[Canon IV of Gangra (340 A.D.)]

This is clearly the authentic Apostolic teaching! This venerable Canon condemns the heresy of the Eustathians, the Manichees, and others who forbade the married priests to celebrate the Liturgy. But see how quickly it is forgotten by the Council of Carthage:

"It has been decided that as regards these three ranks which have been conjoined by a certain bond of chastity and sacerdocy (I am referring particularly to Bishops, Presbyters, and Deacons), as befits devout Bishops and Priests of God, and Levites, and those ministering to divine institutions, they must be continent in all things, so as to be able to obtain whatever in general they ask God for, in order that we too may likewise keep what has been handed down through the Apostles and has been held ever since the early days."—[Canon III of Carthage (419 A.D.)]

"It is decided that Bishops, Presbyters, and Deacons, and all men who handle sacred articles, being guardians of sobriety, must abstain from women."—[Canon IV of Carthage]

This is precisely the erroneous Roman discipline, which required ordinands to *"solemnly promise to have no further intercourse with their wives,"* and which was completely condemned by Canon XIII of the 6th Ecumenical Council. It was carried from Rome to Africa by Bishop Faustinus of Picenum, the legate of the Pope of Rome and the man who proposed this Canon IV of Carthage. The absolute premise of these Canons is that women are unclean, a tenet which is blasphemous and heretical, as discussed above, not to mention being proof of the perpetrator's misagomy and misogyny. The reasoning follows that, if women are unclean, then to touch a woman sexually defiles a man and makes him unfit for sacred service. So much for the Word of God! So much for *Marriage is honorable in all, and the bed undefiled [Hebrews 13:4].*

"It is decreed that Subdeacons who attend to the Mysteries, and Deacons and Presbyters, and even Bishops, on the same terms, must abstain from their wives, so as to be as though they had none; which if they fail to do they shall be removed from office. As for the rest of the Clerics, they shall not be compelled to do this, unless they be of an advanced age; but the rule ought to be kept in accordance with the custom of each particular church."—[Canon XXXIII of Carthage]

This Canon distinguishes between crypto-celibacy on the one hand, and real marriage on the other hand. It commands unnatural *crypto-celibacy*—the clergy continuing to cohabit with their wives, but doing so without having intimate relations. This promotion of unnatural marital relations is totally out of conformity with Holy Scripture. (Note that, even in such an anti-marital Canon as this one, the implication is clear that Bishops have wives: *"and even Bishops, on the same terms, must abstain from their wives…".*)

Canon XII of the 6th Ecumenical Council is, at best, anomalous. While I will not condemn Canon XII nor any jurisdiction which continues to follow that Canon, I believe we Orthodox should be permitted to follow the still-standing, never-revoked, God-pleasing Canons V and LI of the Holy Apostles, and Canon IV of Gangra, which promulgate the discipline which is consistent with the Holy Scriptures: qualified married Priests must be admitted to the sacred episcopate and must be allowed to keep their marriages whole and complete, as intended by almighty God.

Church Divorce for Episcopal Candidates

What the 6th Ecumenical Council intended for the wives of Bishops is made clear in Canon XLVIII of the 6th Ecumenical Council. That Canon provides that women who are wives of Priests about to become Bishops and their husbands must first divorce by common consent and, after his consecration, she is to enter a convent; if she is worthy, she may be ordained a Deaconess. Given the high office of the episcopate, there is real reason to expect some degree of coercion of candidates' wives to cooperate, so as not to block their advancement in the Church hierarchy. I believe that this should be considered to be the rule, rather than the exception, given the human realities of such situations.

Furthermore, remembering that our Lord said, *"What therefore God hath joined together, let not man put asunder,"* we should not actively promote this practice, lest Priests abuse the right and coerce their wives into entering convents. In fact, remembering that a married couple are *one flesh* in the eyes of God [Genesis 2:24], even truly voluntary divorces for this purpose should not be permitted to all who request them. Nonetheless, because there are those rare married couples who honestly and piously both wish to enter into the Angelic vocation, and where the prayerful discernment of the Bishop may find that, for that particular couple, such a course would more likely work toward their ultimate salvation, we ought to allow, very rarely, an exception so that husband and wife may become monastics. The Bishop examining such a case should be extraordinarily attentive to the real motivations of the wife and to the likelihood of coercion by the husband.

In summary, the hierarchy should admonish the clergy of every rank that they must keep their marriages whole and complete, honorable and undefiled, as intended by almighty God, and that they must not harm their marriages in any way on the pretext of reverence because they are *"in the Sacerdotal List."* While voluntary celibacy is a wonderful thing, the idea that marriage is in any respect unclean must be attacked whenever it arises, as the blasphemous heresy that it is.

Married Bishops—First Line of Defense Against Monastic Excesses and Heresy

It bears repeating once more: When those most prone to falling into *neo-Manichaeism* are also the sole hierarchs of the Church (that is, the exclusively-monastic episcopate), the danger of further distorting Christian Faith in favor of *neo-Manichaeism* obviously is very great. Since virtually all Bishops have been monks for over a thousand years, the reversal of this erroneous progression into heresy will occur only by a great movement of the Holy Spirit. The monastic hierarchy now teaches that the *Angelic vocation* of monasticism is superior to the vocation of marriage. This kind of excess scandalizes the faithful. Every person who knows the Scriptures knows that **the union of man and woman is God's plan** [Genesis 1:26-28; 2:21-25]. They know what the New Testament says: *"Marriage is honorable in all, and the bed undefiled"* [Hebrews 13:4]; *"What therefore God hath joined together, let not man put asunder"* [Matthew 19:6].

To say that the monastic vocation, invented by holy men and women inspired by Our Lord Jesus Christ, however excellent it may be, is superior to God's own

plan for men and women—that is scandalous. To back up this excessive evalua-
tion of monasticism with misagomous and misogynous arguments and offensive
disparagement of women and marriage—that is scandalous. To ignore the
human problems that can and sometimes do arise in the unnatural state of
monastic life, such as homosexual behaviours, phobic attitudes toward women,
and so forth, while extolling monasticism as superior to married life—that is
scandalous. To legislate (as the sole legislators) changes from the Apostolic
Church discipline to force the laity to follow ascetic monastic lifestyles (like the
excessive fasting rules now in force in all traditionalist jurisdictions)—that is
scandalous. To deceptively disparage married Bishops as *false Bishops and no Bishops at all*, knowing full well that the married episcopate was normative in the
Apostolic Church and for centuries thereafter—that is scandalous. After so many
centuries, these scandals have not been without their corrosive effect on the faithful.

The few married Bishops now remaining in the Orthodox Churches are, in fact,
the first line of defense against the proponents of misagomy and misogyny, of
neo-Manichaen heresy and blasphemy. In their persons, they and their wives
embody the Christian truth, that God made man male and female and that all
things God made are exceedingly good. They show what a heresy it is to say that
the body is evil and that a woman defiles a man. They are witnesses of God's plan
for the propagation of the race of mankind, the heterosexual relationship of man
and wife; the exclusively-monastic episcopate cannot make this witness.

The issue of the married Bishops is far from being a minor matter of Church discipline, long-since resolved and no longer relevant or important. To the contrary,
this is a very urgent matter of the greatest importance to the Church of Jesus
Christ, for, if such a fundamental heresy as *neo-Manichaeism* cannot be overcome, if it continues to seduce the minds and hearts of most of the Orthodox
episcopate, then the central Church organizations, the *visible Church*, will one
day be found to be apostate. The *visible Church* will be an heretical organization,
no better than the Manichees, no better than the Gnostics, fit only as a bride for
Anti-Christ. The Church has been in the catacombs before, in the beginning of
the Christian era, and in this century. It may go to the catacombs again, if that is
the only place where genuine Christianity can survive. If we do go back to the
catacombs, you can be sure that the Bishops will be married men, not careerist
monks.

As I said earlier, when Abp. Aftimios married, it catalyzed the active reconsideration in Holy Church of the issue of the married episcopate. Once the issue was publicly raised, the discovery of the scriptural truth and the reaffirmation of the Apostolic teaching became more possible. This question of the married episcopate has been posed, not only academically, nor only in the context of proposals for canonical legislation, but it has been embodied and lived in sacrificial Christian witness by Abp. Aftimios and Mariam Ofiesh, and by the many Bishops and their co-suffering wives who followed in their courageous example, acting out of conviction that the married episcopate is truly Scriptural. Abp. Aftimios' desire to force the issue of the married episcopate to consideration by a Pan-Orthodox Council was thwarted in 1933, but by the grace of God, it may yet be fulfilled.

Humbly submitted by Denis M. Garrison, January 1996.

"Marriage is honorable in all, and the bed undefiled:..." [Hebrews 13:4]

"What therefore God hath joined together, let not man put asunder." [Matthew 19:6]

"No Bishop, Presbyter, or Deacon shall put away his own wife under pretext of reverence. If, however, he put her away, let him be excommunicated; and if he persist in so doing, let him be deposed from office." [Canon V of the Holy Apostles]

"If any Bishop, or Presbyter, or Deacon, or anyone at all on the sacerdotal list, abstains from marriage, or meat, or wine, not as a matter of mortification, but out of an abhorrence thereof, forgetting that all things are exceedingly good, and that God made man male and female, and blasphemously misrepresenting God's work of creation, either let him mend his ways or let him be deposed from office and expelled from the Church. Let a layman be treated similarly." [Canon LI of the Holy Apostles]

"If anyone discriminates against a married Presbyter, on the ground that he ought not to partake of the offering when that Presbyter is conducting the Liturgy, let him be anathema." [Canon IV of Gangra (340 A.D.)]

APPENDIX B

My Relations with the Protestant Episcopal Church

by Archbishop Joseph Rene Vilatte

The Introduction to this work is given by Mar Georgius I, the patriarch of Glastonbury et al. [Mar Georgius I, (H.G. de Willmott Newman)—Joseph Renee Vilatte, Glastonbury, London, UK, 1960]

Joseph Rene Vilatte was born at Paris, France, on the 24th of January 1854, and on 7th June 1885 was ordained to the sacred priesthood by Monsignor Edward Herzog, Old Catholic Bishop of Berne, Switzerland. He was consecrated to the Episcopate on 29th May 1892 by Archbishop Antonio Francisco Xaverier Alverez of the Independent Catholic Church of Ceylon, Goa and India. As Archbishop of The Old Catholics of America. Monsignor Vilatte operated in the area of Lake Michigan for some 40 years. In his old age he returned to his native land France, where he died in 1932, in communion with the Apostolic See of Rome.

So far as his Episcopal career is concerned, this I propose to deal with in a forthcoming monograph; but until I am able to complete this, and also to more or less pave the way for it, I am publishing Monsignor Vilatte's own work, which amply covers his career as a priest and at least explains, though it does not justify, some of the reasons for that relentless and persistent persecution which Monsignor Vilatte sustained at the hands of the Anglicans until the end of his days and even thereafter.

From Archbishop Vilatte the following facts emerge:

1. In March 1884, entirely upon his own authority, Vilatte, then a layman, started a mission in Green Bay, Wisconsin, among French and Belgian immigrants, of Roman Catholic antecedents.

2. About twelve months later on the suggestion of Pere Hyacinthe of Paris, he contacted the Rt. Rev. J. H. Hobert Brown, Bishop of Fond du Lac in the Protestant Episcopal Church, who became interested in his (Vilatte's) scheme for making this mission an outpost of Old Catholicism.

3. Bishop Brown, after Vilatte had been examined by two of his clergy in theology, recommended him to Monsignor Herzog, Old Catholic Bishop of Berne, for ordination to the priesthood.

4. Wilst awaiting the decision of Bishop Herzog, Bishop Brown tried to persuade Vilatte to accept Anglican ordination, which he refused. On the eve of Vilatte's departure for Europe, he made a further attempt with the same result.

5. On 7th June 1885, when Vilatte was ordained Priest by Bishop Herzog, the latter, instead of administering the Oath of Canonical Obedience the form employed by a Bishop to his Priest, he used the formula "Dost thou promise to the Bishop, thy Ordinary". In view of the fact that by so doing Bishop Herzog discluded jurisdiction over Vilatte, his obligation of obedience, in the absence of any other Old Catholic Bishop having jurisdiction, would automatically become due to the Archbishop of Utrecht, or primus inter pares in the Old Catholic Episcopate.

6. Although certain misleading statements were published in various Anglican newspapers in the years 1885/6/7 to the effect that Vilatte was under the jurisdiction of their Diocese of Fond du Lac, this could not have been the case, inasmuch as Vilatte at no time fulfilled the conditions required for incardination into the ministry of the Protestant Episcopal Church, inasmuch as he never subscribed the Declaration provided by Article 7 of the Constitution of the Protestant Episcopal Church.

7. Notwithstanding the foregoing, Vilatte did agree to Bishop Brown including his name in the Diocesan clergy list, understanding this as an honorary distinction.

8. Vilatte did solicit donations to his missions using as his testimonial a letter from Bishop Brown, dated 16th September 1887, whereupon no mention was made of the Protestant Episcopal Church.

{Bishop Brown died May 2, 1888}

9. Bishop Brown having died 2nd May 1888, he was on 13th November, succeeded in the Anglican See of Fond du Lac by Charles Chapman Grafton, who, realizing that Vilatte's missions were Old Catholic and nothing to do with the Protestant Episcopal Church, persuaded him to transfer them to the Trustees of the Diocese of Fond du Lac, to be held in trust for Old Catholicism, in return for which the Trustees apparently financed them, and paid Vilatte a stipend. This was a fatal mistake on the part of Vilatte.

10. Monsignor Heykamp, Archbishop of Utrecht, to whom Vilatte owed canonical obedience, having been made aware of this extraordinary position and relations between Vilatte and the Diocese of Fond du Lac, wrote him on the 19th September 1889. Urging him to sever connection. By letter dated 8th October 1889, Monsignor Dipendaal, Bishop of Deventer, a suffragan of Utrecht, wrote Vilatte in similar strain. From these and subsequent letters, and also from letters from Professor Van Thiel, and other Dutch priests, it is clear the Church of Holland regarded Vilatte as their protégé, and leader of an Old Catholic movement in the USA, and not under the jurisdiction of the Protestant Episcopal Church.

11. In April 1890, Vilatte informed Grafton of the letters he had received from Holland, and during the discussion the question of his consecration first came up for particle consideration. Dr. Grafton eventually persuaded Vilatte to let him approach Archbishop Heykamp.

12. By his letter to Archbishop Heykemp, dated April 1890, Grafton commenced his attacks upon Vilatte, not scrupling to make veiled threats towards His Grace, and to tell deliberate lies.

13. By letter dates 14th April 1890, Grafton offered to transfer Vilatte to either Heykemp or Herzog; which if there had been a genuine misconception on either side, would have been the correct thing to do.

14. By letter dated 14th April 1890, Monsignor Heykemp ruled that even if Vilatte had taken an oath of obedience to Fond du Lac, as a Catholic priest, he ought to sever any relationships.

15. Grafton, meanwhile, was continuing his vilification of Vilatte, and on 8th August 1890 wrote a letter to the Russian Orthodox Church, Bishop Vladimir in an attempt to disturb the harmonious relations which existed between him and Vilatte.

16. In the interim, it had been arranged that a proposal for the consecration of Vilatte, as Old Catholic Bishop of the United States, should be considered by the forthcoming Old Catholic Congress at Cologne.

17. In September 1890, Grafton, writing to the Anglican newspapers, warned Protestant Episcopalians not to donate money to Vilatte, who on 19th September formally withdrew connection.

18. At the Old Catholic Congress at Cologne in September 1890, it was decided that it was not expedient to proceed with the proposed consecration of Vilatte.

19. Being served from Fond du Lac, and abandoned by the Old Catholics, who had encouraged him to take that step, Vilatte, through Bishop Vladimir, opened up negations with the Russian Holy Governing Synod, meanwhile being taken under Vladimir's protection.

20. By letter of 23rd October 1890, Vilatte wrote informing the Archbishop of Utrecht that he had been taken under the protection of the Russian Orthodox Church, and would therefore require nothing further from Utrecht.

21. On 20th February 1891, Grafton purported to suspend Vilatte, not withstanding that he was under the protection of Vladimir.

22. Meanwhile Vilatte had got into contact with Archbishop Alvarez of Ceylon, to whom he explained his position and difficulties; and who, by letter dated 10th May 1891 wrote offering to confer the Episcopate upon Vilatte.

23. No decision having been reached by the Russian Synod, Vilatte accepted the offer of Alvarez, and departed for Ceylon, where he remained for some months.

24. On 29th March 1892, Grafton purported to depose Vilatte from the priesthood.

25. On 29th of May 1892, Vilatte was consecrated Old Catholic Bishop of America by Archbishop Alvarez.

It is difficult to see from the foregoing record anything which can be charged to Father Vilatte's discredit. It is equally clear that it fully disposes of Grafton's claim that Vilatte was never under his jurisdiction. Accordingly Grafton had no right to depose him, or even suspend him.

That there was some sort of an informal association between the Vilatte missions and the Diocese of Fond du Lac is certain; but it was in the first instance exceedingly loose and ill-defined. It is possible that Vilatte, who for many years was not too facile with his English, might have misconstrued remarks of Bishop Brown, or that the latter may have misconstrued the remarks of Vilatte. One would prefer to think no, in order to clear Bishop Brown, who seems to have been a kindly old soul. But the position with regard to Bishop Grafton admits no question of misunderstanding. By his crafty scheme to get control of Vilatte's missions, and by various letters he wrote, he reveals his duplicity.

It is certain:

a) If Vilatte was under the jurisdiction of Fond du Lac, then Grafton would have been entitled to depose him.

b) If, on the other hand, Vilatte was not under Grafton's jurisdiction, then whosoever jurisdiction was in fact under notwithstanding, Grafton had no power to suspend or depose him.

The matter is settled for all time: Vilatte at no time subscribed the Declaration required by the Canon Law of the Protestant Episcopal Church to be subscribed by clergy ordained outside that church.

Until he did so, he could not, legally or canonically, become a Presbyter of the Protestant Episcopal Church. He was therefore, at no time under the jurisdiction of the Bishop of Fond du Lac, Consequently, Grafton had no right or power to depose him; and his propertied act of deposition was illegal, and ineffective. His persecution of Violate, therefore, lacks even the poor excuse that Vilatte had laid himself open to it by being a disloyal Presbyter of his (Grafton) diocese; and rests upon no other foundation then hatred, malice and all uncharitableness.

On this unpleasant note ends Monsignor Vilatte's relationship with the Protestant Episcopal Church; though the persecution did not end. But that is another story, which I hope to tell later.

In conclusion, I would like to say, that presenting Archbishop Vilatte's MS to the public, my duty has compelled me to make drastic criticisms of Anglicanism generally, and of Bishop Grafton in particular. So far as the latter is concerned, his letters and actions speak for themselves, and the reader will be well able to judge for himself weather or not my criticisms have been justified. Anglicanism can only be judged by the acts of its representatives. But least any should imagine that I have some deep-seated animosity against that body, I would make it clear that such is not the case.

Although the actions of Anglicanism towards Archbishops Vilatte, and Mathew, and Bishop Herford and others, have frankly disgusted me, and caused me to reverse that favorable opinion which formally I had of it; and although I have been disillusioned regarding its claims to Orders, Missions and Jurisdiction, I do not bear it any personal ill-will. Indeed, I take this opportunity to testify to the fact that had the Anglican Church failed to survive the attacks by the Puritans of the 17th century, there is still little doubt that Britain would have lapsed into ultimate agnosticism or even atheism; for whatsoever her imperfections from the Catholic standpoint, Anglicanism has kept alive some conception of a Church of Episcopacy, and of Liturgical Worship, and of the Catholic Creeds. For this we are truly indebted.

Is it to much to hope that the Anglican Communion will at long last recognize that every man is by law entitled to worship God in his own way. Without let, hindrance, attack and vilification? So far as Britain is concerned, with a population of nearly 50 million churchless souls, there is surely room in the vineyard for bishops and priests of non Ultramontane Catholicism?

+Georgius

Patriarch of Glastonbury.

MY RELATIONS WITH THE PROTESTANT EPISCOPAL CHURCH

Archbishop Joseph Rene Vilatte

The question of my relations with the Episcopal Church in America has been the subject of correspondence, explanation and strife almost from the beginning of my work as an Old Catholic Missionary. In dealing with this question, I, in my experience with Christian Bishops, believed always that the only defense necessary was a statement of simple truth concerning the question at issue. How I have fared as a result of the following faithfully this principle, the entire world knows. When I was attacked openly by Bishop Grafton and his party I defended myself so well as I could by publishing extracts from his letters to refute the charges brought against me. He, however, when silenced on one point, would always change his position and raise a new issue. Fortunately, for myself, I had preserved every letter of importance written by persons bearing on my relations with the Episcopal Church, and the Old Catholics of Europe; and owing to my unconscious foresight, I am able to give you evidence bearing on the question, which has never been published before. I myself, at that time, on account of my unfamiliarity with the English language, was unaware of their great importance in showing how the controversy arose. I found several years ago, a friend who is not only a theologian, but also well versed in civil and church law and to whose research I am indebted for the substance of this defense.

During a short visit last October, he requested me to allow him to examine all my correspondence, beginning with the first missionary work in this country. This search took ten days to complete, and among other documents relating to this question, the once mentioned above, were found. He is studying now in detail the entire matter and has written me that when his work is completed, and given to the world, it will bring about a day of retribution for my enemies, all the more terrible because delayed so long.

To enable you to understand how the controversy arose, I will tell briefly how I became connected with the Protestant Episcopal Church. During the latter part of the Franco-Prussian War, I enlisted in the National Guard, which was defending the City of Paris. When the siege was succeeded by the 'Commune', bringing with it great suffering and want, I determined to leave my native land and sail for Canada, as numerous placards had been posted in the rural districts asking for settlers. Some weeks after arriving in Canada, I learned that a teacher was needed to take charge of a school attached to one of the missions under the direction of a French priest near Ottawa. I took the charge as parish teacher and catchiest, and as the priest visited the mission only once a month, I conducted divine Service on Sunday when the priest was absent. He was pleased with the result of my work that he began to instruct me in Latin. After about two years service I felt a desire to revisit my native land, having received besides a notice from the French Government that I was drafted for a long period of service in the army. When I presented myself to the officers in Paris, I was informed that seven years of service in the army would be required of me. But the spirit of liberty which I had imbibed in America, together with memories of the Franco-Prussian War, made me determined to leave my native land rather then reenter the army.

I went therefore to Belgium and after a few months entered the Community of Christian Brothers, a lay teaching order at Namur. After a year's stay, I felt clearly that my vocation was for the priesthood, and therefore began studying with a professor of Latin for about a year. Then being desirous of returning to Free America, I went to Montreal and presented myself to the Roman Catholic Archbishop Febre of Montreal, who advised me to enter the seminary of Saint Lawrence, where I studied for three years. The teaching of the seminary was rabidly Romanastic that all other beliefs were condemned as heresies, which brought eternal damnation to all who accepted them. During my second vocation, I learned that the famous French priest, Father Chiniquy, was devoting his life to preaching against Roman error, announced in Montreal a series of sermons against Roman error. I attended with great fear several of them and returned to the seminary with my mind much disturbed. After sometime I felt that I could not remain there longer and not knowing what course to peruse. I visited a French Protestant minister in Montreal and after disclosing my state of mind, requested him to advise me. He urged me to join a private class in theology, which he was instructing where I met a French minister who was a professor in McGill University, controlled by the Presbyterians of Canada. He became interested in me and introduced to the President who urged me to continue there my theological studies, which I did, remaining there two years.

After some time, I began to compare Roman Catholicism with Protestantism, and saw plainly that while on the one hand Romanism has added much error and corruption to the primitive faith, Protestantism has not only taken away the Roman errors but also a part of the primitive deposit of faith. Nevertheless, I sought to bring peace to my mind by beginning anew my studies in the Roman Church, and therefore entered as a novice the monastery of the Clerics of Saint

Viateur in Illinois. I had been there about six months when I learned that Father Chiniquy was living near the monastery. I determined to visit him and discuss my perplexities. Father Chiniquy sympathized with me and invited me to remain with him, which I did. After several months of friendship, he advised me not to return to the monastery, but to go to Green bay, Wisconsin, and begin work as a missionary among the French people, who, who although both Protestant and Roman Catholic, were drifting into spiritualism and infidelity. Father Chiniquy also suggested my writing to the famous Father Hyacinthe of Paris, who, as a reformer and fellow Gallican would both sympathize and direct my path. Father Chiniquy wrote to the people of Green bay telling them of my state among them. There reply was a request to come, I therefore took leave of Father Chiniquy and went in March 1884 to that city to begin my labors.

Finding there nothing but factions of different forms of belief, I began visiting various families and urging them to unite and form one congregation and ignore for the present all differences of doctrine. I felt that as long as my own mind was not at rest, I could preach nothing but the simple gospel. Shortly after beginning my work, I wrote Father Hyacinthe of Paris telling him of my situation and state of mind, declaring my conviction that neither Roman Catholicism nor Protestantism would satisfy the spiritual needs of these people who had already abandoned the Roman Church, I requested him to inform me concerning his religious movement in Paris and asked whether council and aid would be given in the effort to establish in America a Catholic church without any other qualification. While waiting for an answer, I conducted Service twice every Sunday and saw my first few listeners increase to a congregation filling the chapel which was enlarged only to be filled again. Under date of September 22, 1884, Pere Hyacinthe wrote that his church held the doctrinal position of the undivided Church before the separation of the East and the West and stated his conviction that if my work were directed by the same principal it would succeed, he also requested information concerning my work in Green Bay. His letter brought peace to my mind because I realized clearly now, where the hope for the future was. I replied to his request for information by stating that there were many hundreds of French and Belgians, a part of whom had already departed the Church, and the remainder, while nominally members, were thoroughly dissatisfied with their Church and therefore I believed that there was a fruitful field for the organization of the purified Catholic Church which would present the Gospel to the people as did the primitive Church, and exercise authority accordingly to the Spirit of free America.

After some months of waiting, Pere Hyacinthe replied on March 14, 1885, by urging me at once to go to Paris to confer with him personally, in the following words:

> "A mistake would be fatal to you and to the important work you propose to undertake. There is much to be said which is impossible to be said by letter. Then your ordination, which should certainly be by the Latin rite, can be easily accomplished by our Old Catholic Bishop of Berne. This is necessary if you hope for any success in the true Catholic reform. If you act with words and charity as becomes a priest of the Holy Church of Christ, you can do a great work, but if you make a false step at the beginning, you will certainly fail, and not only injure your future vocation, but do great harm to the cause of true Catholicism and religious reform. In case you cannot possibly come then you should take advice from the Bishop of the American Episcopal Church of your diocese who is a good and wise man. And you should try by the power of all Christian charity to keep the confidence and love of your people".

As it was impossible for me to leave my newly gathered congregation to consult with Pere Hyacinthe in Paris, I followed his advice by going to the American Bishop Brown, telling him of my intention of beginning a movement of catholic reform among the French speaking people of Green Bay, and showing him the letters of Pere Hyavinthe. Bishop Brown replied to me stating he had heard much concerning my work in Green Bay and would be glad to aid me in this movement. He hoped, furthermore, that in referring this matter to his Standing Committee, that they would understand my particular position, and appreciate the good relationship which would be established between the Episcopal and Old Catholic Church, through me as a medium. Several weeks later I received a letter from Bishop Brown informing me first of all I must take leave of my congregation in Green Bay, after which I was to meet him at the Episcopal Rectory in that city, furthermore that I was to be examined by two of his clergy on my theological education. The examination be satisfactory, Bishop Brown wrote me that he would consult with several of his fellow bishops regarding Pere Hyacinthe's advice that I be ordained by the Old catholic Bishop Herzog. In the meantime I was to go to their seminary at Nashotah and remain until a decision was made. Several weeks after coming to Nashotah, I wrote to pere Hyacinthe informing him of my position, and two days later, I wrote to Bishop Herzog of Berne, requesting him to ordain me.

After one month's waiting I received the following letter from Bishop Brown, dated April 27, 1885.

> "I have submitted the suggestion of Pere Hyacinthe, that you go to Berne for ordination, to the judgment and advice of our bishops and am satisfied that it is the wisest course for you and all interested to be pursued".

One week later, I received from his letter, dated May 5, 1885.

> "The Standing Committee of the diocese have just met. After full discussion of your matter they have put into my hands testimonials warranting your ordination to the diaconate immediately and to the priesthood as soon afterwards as possible. The main reason controlling the Standing Committee were the conviction that the Anglican succession off Apostolic authority is preferable to that of the Old Catholics the importance of maintaining the sufficiency of it in this country, the saving of the time and expense, and a knitting of a closer unity with the diocese from the beginning of the movement."

As soon as I received this letter I went to Fond du Lac and stated to Bishop Brown that I could not accept an Anglican ordination, because it would prevent my work securing the support from the people, that the catholic ordination would insure. For which reason I insisted that he would send at once my certificates to the Old catholic Bishop Herzog of Switzerland. Seeing plainly that I would not accept his ordination, Bishop Brown wrote the following letter, dates May 5, 1885, giving me a copy.

On May 5, 1885, Bishop Brown wrote the following letter to Bishop Herzog.

"The Right Reverend Dr. Herzog,

Bishop of Berne

My dear Brother:

Permit me to introduce to your confidence and esteem the bearer of this letter. Mr. Rene Vilatte, a candidate for Holy Orders in the Diocese of Fond du Lac. Mr. Vilatte is placed in peculiar circumstances. Educated for the priesthood in the Roman Catholic Church he found himself unable to receive the recent Vatican decrees and for a short time associated himself with the Presbyterian communion, but at last, by the mercy of God, was led into council with this branch of the One, Holy, Catholic and Apostolic Church. He resided for a while at Green Bay, a city of this diocese. In the neighborhood of this place there are now settled about 30,000 Belgians. Of these, a large number, probably 8,000, are believed to be inclined to the principals of a pure and primitive Catholicism. Several delegations of these Belgians have waited on Mr. Vilatte and besought him to become their priest. Mr. Vilatte's character for piety, sobriety, purity, intelligence and prudence has been attested to the satisfaction of the authorities of this diocese. Our canons, however, require a longer probation of a candidate the exigency of the circumstances will bear. At the suggestion of Pere Hyacinthe (Loyson) approved by the Bishop of Connecticut, and other Bishops, and by the faculty of Nashotah Seminary, and by me, Mr. Vilatte approaches you to ordain him to the priesthood, as speedily as you can find possible that he may enter upon the great work to which he seems specially summoned. It has been expedient to us to send him to you that he may learn personally something of the aims and spirit of the great movement of which you a recognized leader and to be fitted to cooperate with you in some degree in this country. Mr. Vilatte's _____ means are limited and he desires to be absent from this diocese as short a time as possible. I ask you to ordain him to the priesthood and attest his character, briefly, but sufficiently by saying that I am willing to ordain him, if it should not be expedient to you to do so.

Truly and lovingly your brother and servant, in the Holy Church of Our Lord,

J.H. Hobart Brown
Bishop of Fond du Lac"

As my path was clear of all obstacles, I prepared myself for the journey. Bishop Brown accompanied me to the railroad station, and before leaving me said "I will ordain you a priest tomorrow, if you will be satisfied with your ordination and rest here". To which I replied. "No; Old Catholic I am and Old Catholic I will be". Bishop Brown then assured me that I should never be subject to the Standing Committee of the diocese.

During my absence the following replies to my letters arrived from Pere Hyacinthe and Bishop Herzog.

"Pere Hyacinthe charges me to write you again to say that he has written to Bishop Herzog concerning you, and that if you have made your studies in the Roman Church, and taken the minor orders as we are informed you have, and bringing with you letters of recommendation from the American Episcopal Bishop of your diocese, there is no doubt whatever that Bishop Herzog will confer the priesthood upon you, and this will imply perhaps a residence at Berne for tow or three weeks".

From Bishop Herzog, May 7, 1885:

Dear and honorable Brother:

In reply to your letter of 14th of April, I must tell you that I consider as indispensable, the formal ordination by a Catholic Bishop. I will ordain you a priest with pleasure, but the position I occupy in my country and the relations in which I am placed, face to face with the Bishops of the Episcopal Church of the United States, do not permit me to proceed with your ordination, unless I am authorized formally by the Bishop of the Episcopal Church of the diocese in which your parish is situated.

+ Edward Herzog
Bishop

I arrived in Berne on June 3, and presented the letter from Bishop Brown to Bishop Herzog who requested me immediately to accompany him to Dr. Charles R. Hale, an American Episcopal clergyman who was visiting Berne. Bishop Herzog asked him to examine my testimonials and state his judgment on the matter. Dr. hale replied to Bishop Herzog that of the signers of my papers he knew personally, Dr. Cole, Dr. Adams, and Professor Riley; Professor Kemper alone was a stranger to him. He felt therefore sure that everything was right, and hoped that Bishop Herzog would proceed. Bishop Herzog replied that he would.

The following day, June 4, I was examined by Bishop Herzog, assisted by three priests. On June 5, I received minor orders and the sub-diaconate, on June 6, the diaconate and on June 7, the priesthood.

Concerning my ordination to the priesthood, I wish to call your attention to the following rubrics of the Roman rite of ordination:

"Then each one goes up again to the Bishop and kneeling places his joined hands between those of the Bishop, who says to each, if he be his Ordinary: 'Dost thou promise to me and my successors reverence and obedience'? And he answers "I promise".

"But if the Bishop be not his Ordinary, he says to each secular Priest, while he holds their hands between his own, as aforesaid, 'Dost thou promise to the Bishop, they Ordinary and to his successors, reverence and obedience' and the answer is 'I promise'."

This promise of obedience, as is evident from the rubric, is intended to apply only to ordinations performed by one Roman Bishop for another; it could not be construed to apply to any other ordination. It cannot therefore, be construed into the oath of canonical obedience to the Bishop of Fond du Lac, as the Episcopal Bishop Grafton has stated falsely, and on which his entire contention is based, that I was an Episcopalian clergyman.

On June 13, I sailed for America and arrived at Green Bay on July 3. Soon after my return I began visiting the settlements of French people, and later I obtained a small building in Little Sturgeon which was fitted up as a chapel for regular divine service. On October 16, I was visited for the first time in my parish by Bishop Brown. About a month later Bishop Brown asked me to visit him in Fond du Lac, which I did. During the visit he asked me weather I would permit him to place my name on the Clergy List of the diocese, to which I consented immediately.

In order to enable you to understand how my relations ceased with the Protestant Episcopal Bishop Grafton, which separation resulted in controversy concerning me, with all the falsehoods, slanders and continually repeated attacks on my character and work, I will state briefly now the events that compelled me to take the successive steps resulting in my archiepiscopal consecration, under the Bull of His Holiness Mar Peter Ignatius III, Patriarch of Antioch and all East.

During Bishop Brown's life, my time was occupied entirely in pastoral work, establishing new missions, and soliciting contributions to the aid and support the work, using the following letters of Bishop Brown to introduce myself.

> "Sept 16, 1887
>
> The Reverend Pere Vilatte is about to leave his work at the Mission of the Precious Blood, in quest of funds for the founding and support of the Theological School at Sturgeon Bay, which seems now to be the necessary agent for the extension and perpetuation of his peculiar and most interesting work. From personal observation of Pere Vilatte's labors, I am quite confident that they are undertaken in a spirit of devotion, self-sacrifice, prudence and loyalty to the faith and Order of the Church of Our Lord, which entitles him to the sympathy and aid of loving _____ I bespeak for him a kind and patient hearing.
>
> J.H. Hobart Brown
> Bishop of Fond du Lac"

You will notice the absence of any reference to the Protestant Episcopal Church. This omission is especially noteworthy because its letter was used continually as my authority to collect contributions. While collecting in New York City, I became acquainted with Reverend de Beaumont, a priest who had left the Roman Church several years before. I explained to him the Old Catholic work in Wisconsin, as a result of which, he offered his services as the head of the seminary, the land for which had already been donated. In Chicago, I met Reverend Proth, an ex-Trappist monk, who accompanied me to Little Sturgeon, where I secured a house in the city, which could be used temporarily as a seminary and placed Reverend de Beaumont in charge. About this time, Reverend Oser, a former Swiss parish priest, who with his congregation, was one of the first to join the Old Catholic movement, and whose name was one of the three from which the Old Catholic Bishop of Switzerland was chosen, wrote and asked information concerning my work. I replied, inviting him to visit with me, which he did, remaining about a month. But when he learned of the concoction with the Episcopal diocese of Fond du Lac, he refused to take part in the work. Reverend de Beaumont was introduced by me to Bishop Brown, who after examining his ordination certificate, which I had obtained from the Roman Catholic Bishop Healy of Portland, expressed himself as satisfied. Reverend Proth remained with me until after Bishop Brown's death, collecting money by my authority and with my certificate.

Owing to my ignorance of English, I did not know during these few busy years, that these mis-statements of relations of myself and missions, to the diocese of Fond du Lac, for which Bishop Brown, even though his intention was good, must be considered responsible, were accepted as true by the Episcopal clergy as the extracts given from church papers have shown. In this connection I will mention the oft repeated remark made to me by Bishop Brown "Dear Father: I hope to see you an Old Catholic Bishop"

After Bishop Brown's death on May 2, 1888, my constant fear was that his successor might be a Low Church bishop, who might refuse to aid me in my work. About this time, a letter of inquiry came from Herr Wormhaut, a gentleman of Delft, Holland; who having read in the Dutch paper, an account of my work in Wisconsin wrote me asking further information regarding the movement. I replied by giving him the information requested, and then stated my fears for the future, by saying that Bishop Brown's successor might be a bishop who will not understand the relation of my mission to the diocese of Fond du Lac. That by refusing aid would place insurmountable obstacles in my way, to avoid which, it is evident, we must have a bishop of our own. I stated further that this step need not necessarily in the breaking of the ties which bound us together, but that we could continue to dwell together in charity and love. I closed by requesting Herr Wormhaut to bring this matter of attention to his parish priest (Pastor Harderwyk).

Some weeks after Bishop Brown's death, a French Canadian Christian Brother named Gauthier, whom I had meet during my stat in Montreal, and with whom I had corresponded more or less, offered his services. I received him, and on his arrival, began training him, preparatory for ordination. I have given you these details of my various assistants, in order to show you how much truth there was in the reports (which Bishop Grafton circulated in Europe) of the insignificance of my work, after I, in obedience to the command of Archbishop Heycamp, refused to allow him to administer confirmation to my mission.

On November 13, 1888, Bishop Grafton was chosen to succeed the deceased Bishop Brown. I supported his nomination, believing in view of his well known catholic opinions, that I and my missions would be safe under his protection, until such time as we could secure a bishop of our own. He was consecrated April 25, 1889. {Charles Chapman Grafton, a former "Cowley Father" that is, a member of the Anglican religious order called "The Society of Saint John the Evangelist", was one of the leading High Churchman of his times. He was responsible for the bitter attacks upon Archbishop Vilatte. He died in 1912-DW}

Several weeks after this, I received the following letter from Herr Wormhaut of Delft, in answer to the one I addressed to him, after Bishop Brown's death.

> "Reverend and dear Father,
>
> Nothing in your letter please me so much as your freedom from the milk-and-water theology of Protestantism. But what I don't comprehend is your desire, even if you had the Old Catholic succession to be in perfect communion with the Protestant Episcopal Church, for you surly must be aware of the fact that the whole Catholic church, both the East and the West, including our own national branch, consider her orders exceedingly doubtful. Some of her own members, both lay and clerical, participate in this doubt, and have in England banded themselves together into a society known as the Order of Corporate Reunion, as for the doctrine of the Anglican Church, it is undoubtedly heretical, and heresy is heresy, whether found in the Book of Common Prayer or in the decrees of the Vatican".

Very soon after I received this letter, the following letter dated June 4, 1889, came from pastor Hyderwyk.

"When you write to Herr Wormhaut that it is necessary for you to have a bishop in perfect communion with the American Episcopal Church, I must say that to such a position and proposition, I could never subscribe. For (1st) The American Episcopal Church is not Catholic in doctrine, her faith in the holy sacraments (of which the Catholic Church numbers seven) is in no wise that of the primitive church. The doctrine of the American Episcopal Church, as well as that of the Church of England, touching to the holy sacraments of the altar and the sacrifice of Jesus Christ in the Eucharist, is positively Protestant. (2nd) The Apostolic Succession and validity of the Episcopal consecration in England and America is extremely doubtful. Perhaps you will say: The Old Catholics of Germany and Switzerland are in communion with Anglicans. It is true. But I believe the prelates in Germany and Switzerland are led astray by the specious sayings of individual bishops without being at all at one with the Anglican Church in general".

Sometime after his consecration, Bishop Grafton, visited me during the summer of 1889 at Little Sturgeon, when I presented Brother Gauthier to him, and stated that I intended to have him ordained by Bishop Herzog, without consulting anyone else connected with the Episcopal diocese. Bishop Grafton consented and requested me to write to Bishop Herzog concerning the ordination, stating that he would also write to him.

In discussing the financial questions relating to the support of the missions, I stated to him that I thought it necessary to go and collect money to pay the debt of our new church, as after Bishop Brown's death, I had sold many things belonging to me, even my watch, to pay the workmen. Bishop Grafton replied: "No; I would be the beggar for Old Catholicism; donate your missions to the Diocese of Fond du Lac, and the trustees will pay your debt; for I do not wish you to make appeals yourself" But when I accessed, I gave the property to the Diocese of Fond du Lac on the condition that it should be for the use of Old Catholicism, hence it would be no more diverted to the use of the Protestant Episcopal Church then to the Methodists.

Bishop Herzog replied to Bishop Grafton's request as follows:

"Berne, August 20, 1889.

To: The Right Reverend Charles C. Grafton
Bishop of Fond du Lac

My Lord,

Accept, first of all, my cordial wishes of congratulation and benediction on your elevation to the Episcopate. The news I received of your election and consecration was an evidence to me, how peculiarly fortunate the Diocese of Fond du Lac should consider itself to have procured your person, so distinguished a successor to the memorable Bishop Brown. I thank you, too especially the kindly disposition which you manifest towards Vilatte and his work. It rejoices my heart, that in your episcopal visitation you have made satisfactory observation and regard to the movement as deserving your entire support. It will afford me great pleasure to conform to your wish to supply an assistant to ___ Vilatte by conferring priestly ordination upon the Rev. J. B. Gauthier. Rev. Dr. Hale, Dean of Davenport, who was present at the ordination of Vilatte at Berne, has made it clear to me, why it would be advantageous that the ordination should be performed by me.

I am most worthy Bishop
Your devoted,

Edward Herzog,
Bishop

In this connection, I want to call your attention to the underlines sentence in Bishop Herzog's letter {it was not underlined "that in your Episcopal visitation you must have made satisfactory observation and regard the movement as deserving your entire support" in part 12]} which show plainly that at this time, I and the mission were not considered a part of, or under the jurisdiction of the Episcopal Diocese of Fond du Lac.

On September 6, 1889, I received a letter from Bishop Grafton containing among other things the following: "Bishop Herzog's most satisfactory and cheerful epistle shows that Brother Gauthier must depart soon to meet him. I have sent a copy of this letter to Brother Gauthier. See that this matter does not get into the papers. There is one matter that I want you and Brother Gauthier to be cheerful of. Study as to how you can keep yourselves and your affairs out of the newspapers. Don't let anything said prompt you to reply. Let the world and the Church and the Romans think we have failed and died out. let us study how we can keep hidden for a few years. Do not let the opening of the monastery be a public matter".

It is evident to everyone that Bishop Grafton realized at this time that the proposed ordination of Brother Gauthier by Bishop Herzog, like my own, was one which by its very nature placed him beyond any canonical jurisdiction of the Bishop of Fond du Lac. If this were not so, there would be no reason for keeping the knowledge of his Church, the steps by which this ordination was obtained. This fact, is proof that Bishop Grafton realized even more clearly then did Bishop Brown, that I was, accordingly to the canon law of the Protestant Episcopal Church, independent of the Bishop of Fond du Lac.

Bishop Herzog's reply being satisfactory to all concerned, I gave Brother Gauthier the necessary money to go to Berne, and on his return, I assigned him to the mission in Little Sturgeon, as I had removed to the new mission at Duval, a few weeks before Bishop Brown's death. In answering the letter of Pastor Harderwyk of June 4, 1889, I told him among other things of the steps I had taken to have Brother Gauthier ordained by Bishop Herzog and stated that on account of our poverty, I would be unable to continue sending young men to Bishop Herzog for ordination, for which reason, if for no other, it is absolute necessary that we have a bishop as soon as possible. I concluded by saying that if the bishops of Holland prefered to consecrate one of their own priests our bishop, instead of conferring the episcopate on me, that I would be entirely satisfied.

Pastor Harderwyk replied with the following letter:

"Delft, Holland
September 11, 1889

You must disentangle yourself from the Protestant Episcopal Church. For that reason you have acted prudently in not having Mr. Gauthier ordained priest by Bishop Grafton, who had, to say the least, a doubtful, if not invalid consecration. It is impossible for you, who are a Catholic, to remain under the jurisdiction of a Bishop (?) who is, seriously speaking, Protestant and whose apostolic succession is very doubtful. For this reason, I counsel you to separate yourself totally from the Episcopal Church. You will say then, that it is absolutely necessary for you to have a truly Catholic Bishop" he goes on to say "I do not doubt that our bishops will participate with you once you have disconnected yourself from the Protestant Episcopal Church and that the Old Catholic Church in America would be a daughter of the Church in Holland".

Some weeks before, I had written to Archbishop Heykamp of Utrecht, telling him of my movement for Catholic reform and its connection with the Episcopal Diocese of Fond du Lac. His reply to my letter, came several weeks after the last one I received from Pastor Harderwyk, and reads as follows.

"Utrecht,
September 19, 1889

To. Reverend Rene Vilaltte
Priest over the Old Catholics in America.

We received with great joy your protestation of being, and wishing, to remain free from all Protestant influences; for what is a dangerous stumbling block over which so many have fallen, when seeing the deplorable state in which the Church of Christ is found, they have risen up against the profane novelties introduced, and opposed themselves to unltramontanism. We also note with great joy that you do not make common cause with the Anglicans, who, leaving aside the validity of their orders, at bottom are not Catholics, but Protestants. For this reason, we hope that, however painful may be your situation, you will not rest in ecclesiastical communion with them, nor ever accept from them any religious service. It is better, in the wilderness where divine providence has led us, to abandon ourselves wholly to God then to implore the spiritual succor of those who are not united with us in the same faith in the truth which is one.

The Church of Holland recognizes the Roman Church as the only true Church of Jesus Christ, and the Pope of Rome as the Center of Catholic unity. Whoever occupies the See of Rome as long as the supreme tribunal of the Catholic Church has not condemned him, the Church of Holland regards as vested with the primacy in the church. She respects the character with which he is invested, but does not obey him in that which is contrary to truth and the spirit of the holy gospel. She, by the Grace of God, remains in the Roman Church and abhors schism as the greatest crime of the Church. Thus, by unmerited grace, the Church of Holland guards a sound and correct position in the Roman Catholic Church.

I salute you and your brothers with all my heart,
Your humble and devoted servant,

John Heykamp
Archbishop of Utrecht

Bishop Grafton came to visit me about this time, and during his stay, I showed him the letters which I had received from Herr Wormbout, pastor Harderwyk,

Archbishop Haykamp and Bishop Diespendaal, explaining how I came to begin the correspondence. Bishop Grafton said nothing in reply, but as the following letter from Archbishop Heykemp, dated December 21, 1889, plainly shows, he must have decided at that early time, on his plan of action; which was to make the Bishops of Holland believe that my work was so insignificant, that a bishop was utterly unnecessary.

> "You may well conceive, dear Father, that we would in no manner have it understood that from the human and material assistance, you should remain in harmony and ecclesiastical relationship with a church whose faith is not Catholic, and which is, separate from the center of Catholic unity. We had thought of you as though there were certain priests who had chosen your side; we now have learned 'that they are Anglican ministers' who quitted you later on, regretting the opinions and leeks of Egypt, ie: creature comforts of the Anglican Church and not willing to share with you a more modest situation.
>
> Whatever the future may be my dear Father, do not loose courage; the cause you have the happiness to defend this cause of God.
>
> John Haykemp
>
> Archbishop of Utrecht"

Early in the year 1890, I compiled and had printed our Confession of Faith, sending a copy to Bishop Grafton, to Archbishop Haykemp of Utrecht, and to Bishop Vladimir, the Russian Bishop of Alaska. I could not possibly have dared to do this, had I been at the time, or considered myself an Episcopal minister. The reason for this statement is obvious by reading Article 7 of the Constitution of the Protestant Episcopal Church.

The Following letter from Professor van Thiel, the President of the Old Catholic Seminary at Amersfoort, is very interesting.

> "I am happy to assure you that the reading of your 'Sketch' has quite satisfied me. It has rejoiced me so much the more in that, while altogether respecting your apostolic zeal, I believed there was some subject for fear lest your church ran the risk of departing from the true Catholic doctrine. For firstly, I know your ministry was connected, though even so slightly, with the Anglican diocese; then, in an account of Old Catholic work, I read among other things 'although the creed or doctrine be the same, our Old Catholic ritual is entirely different from the Episcopal liturgy' nevertheless, I know that the doctrine of the Episcopal Church differs in essential points from that of the Catholic Church, But, now happily the profession of faith you have published leaves no

doubt whatever, that your missionary church is altogether conformed to the ancient faith of the Catholic Church, and that she is determined to cling closely thereto. Your profession appears to me to be very clear and assuredly, as to its doctrine, we should have no difficulty subscribing to it. I understand that you will keep yourself and your students, as much as possible, in conformity with our doctrinal education and practice of the Church of Utrecht, which you like to consider as your spiritual mother; to whom you are very intimately attached, and of the Catholic purity of whose doctrine you are entirely convinced. I rejoice with all my heart in your good intention. I need not say to you that in the meantime, I am ready to give you as much aid, advice and information, as is in my power. However I pray that the Lord may bless the work of your Mission, and that nothing will prevent our Church from procuring for you very soon the spiritual aid you need. Accept the affectionate and respectful sentiments of,

Yours devotedly,

C.J. van Thiel
Amersfoort"

APPENDIX C

A Brief Biographical Section on Mar Julius I

By John Philip Kottapparambil, Kottayam, India
Reproduced by Permission

Fr. Alwarez of Roman Catholic Church joins the Jacobite Syrian Orthodox Church of Antioch.

Fr. Alwarez was born in a Roman Catholic family at Goa. After completing his studies from the *'Real Seminary'* of Rakkol, at the age of 30 in 1860, he joined the Jesuits Missionary at Bombay. Though he remained with them for many years, he was disillusioned with their activities and so he returned to his native place. After reaching Goa, he started an orphanage and later a college. He was a known social worker. During his stay there, he published some periodicals and through this he criticised the misgivings of the Jesuit Missionaries which was a known fact at that time. On seeing these articles, Archbishop of Goa excommunicated him from the Roman Catholic Church and he was forced to leave the place due to the continuous persecution against him risen out of the vengeance. He later escaped to Travancore.

During his stay at Travancore he came to know more about the Apostolic Suriyani Church of Antioch. He was attracted towards it. Meanwhile he started a movement namely "Swathantra Catholic Mission" and through this, opposed the atrocities of the Roman Catholic Church. Later Dr. Lisbowa Pinto, a member of this movement with other like minded people of the Catholic Church started a periodical, "Independent Catholic" published from Colombo. Many others were also convinced in the Apostolic Episcopacy of the Syrian Orthodox Church. Around the time, Fr. Alwareaz who was in regular contact with the Patriarch of Antioch, met Malankara Metropolitan Mor Dionysius V (Pulikottil Thirumeni) on His Holiness request. With the permission of the Patriarch, Mor Gregorius Geevarghese (Parumala Kochu Thirumeni) consecrated Fr. Alwarez as a Ramban of the Syrian Orthodox Church. On Monday the 29th July 1889, the Ramban was consecrated as 'Metropolitan' at the Kottayam old Seminary chapel by Malankara Metropolitan *Mor Dionysius V* and assisted by other Metropolitans including our Kochu Thirumeni. The new Metropolitan Alwarez Mor Julius was given the charge of the new Mangalore and Bombay dioceses. Later many people, particularly the disillusioned Roman Catholics from other parts of India and Ceylon joined the Syrian Church. Under the influence of the new Metropolitan, many from the old Catholic Church of America including one Rev. J Rene Vilatte, a French Priest, joined the Church.

Later on the advice of Metropolitan Alwarez Mor Julius, the Patriarch of Antioch gave permission for the consecration of Rev. Rene Vilatte as a Metropolitan. The ceremony was planned at the St. Mary's Church, Colombo. On the Ascension day (26th May) in 1892, Rev. J Rene Vilatte was elevated as a Ramban and three days later, he was consecrated as Metropolitan 'Mor Thimothious', by Kadavil Paulose Mor Athanasious of Kottayam diocese, our Kochu Thirumeni of Niranam diocese and Alwarez Mor Julius. The new Metropolitan, Mor Thimothious was appointed as the Archbishop of American diocese under the Holy See of Antioch. This was an eventful day for the Universal Syrian Church. The expense of the ceremony was shared by the representative of the American government in Colombo. In a special function that followed, the governmental authorities awarded a rare title of *"Commander of the Crown of Thorns"* to the three Metropolitans including our Kochu Thirumeni.

In all the discussions with the newly converted Metropolitans, Parumala Mor Gregorious Bawa (together with Pulikottil Thirumeni and Kadavil Thirumeni) participated as an intermediary. It was he who contacted and informed about the latest developments to the Patriarch. Many such decisions regarding Malankara Church were taken by the Patriarch Ignatius Peter III, mainly on the advice our Kochu Thirumeni. Both were in constant contact, until the last days of the Patriarch.

0-595-28407-8

Printed in the United States
62854LVS00003B/159

9 780595 284078